GOOD NEWS
FOR THOSE WHO WONDER

Dr. J. Michael Miller

DEDICATION

As I wrote, I was conscious of the presence of my beloved teacher, mentor and friend, the late Dr. Harrell F. Beck, who, in my years at Boston University School of Theology, inspired in me and many others a deep love for the Bible, particularly the Old Testament. This book is, I hope, a reflection of his joy and is dedicated to him.

CONTENTS

Acknowledgments   v

Introduction   vii

1   How It All Began   1

2   A Lot of People and a Law   13

3   Some Kind of Government   27

4   The Government's Critics   43

5   A Unique Person   59

6   Out of This World   73

7   Post Script   87

About the Author   91

J MICHAEL MILLER

ACKNOWLEDGMENTS

I am ever grateful to my friends in an Editing Group, Scotty Brewington, Tony Cobourn and Rev. Jody Vickery, for their careful suggestions and criticisms. Their work has immensely improved this book.

Biblical quotations are taken from the New Revised Standard Version. In order to keep the flow of the text, I have deliberately avoided inserting notations of the precise biblical sources.

J MICHAEL MILLER

INTRODUCTION

This is a book for those who have walked by any number of churches, but seldom entered. It is for those who have wandered into a Christian bookstore and been overwhelmed by the number of Bibles on display. You may know some of the stories of the Bible, but have never read more than a few passages. You wonder what the Bible is about and why people bother to join churches and call themselves "Christians."

I have studied the Bible much of my adult life and still marvel at its complexities. I believe the basic story of my faith is there, but it is buried under details and interpretations that tend to obscure that story.

Most of my life, I have been involved in the activities of the church. Sometimes I think that churches do more to make the biblical stories confusing than to illuminate them. Not that I think the normal church activities – worship services, baptisms, weddings and funerals – are unimportant. For the people participating, the activities are very important. Biblical passages are read frequently, but the people in church assume everyone knows the basic stories. These stories, however, are very distant in time and setting from our daily life. Church people often talk about things that do not easily connect with our every day routine.

So what are the Bible's stories and what is this "Christianity" that seems so important to those who call themselves "Christians"? Let's start with the first three words of the Bible—"In the beginning."

J MICHAEL MILLER

1

HOW IT ALL BEGAN

"In the beginning" – these are the opening words of the Bible. Not very original. The opening line should certainly have been more grand for a collection of books that has had such a great influence on the history of the world. But the Bible generally avoids flowery language.

The first thing the Bible talks about is how the world began, but it doesn't resemble the story told by modern physicists and astronomers. That's because none of the authors of the Bible were scientists. They didn't know about the discoveries of mathematicians and archaeologists. All they knew was what they observed. They saw the sun rise in the morning and set at night.

They knew that the seasons changed. Some months were warmer than others. They knew they had to plant seeds at a certain time so that the crops would grow. They understood that it was necessary to water the young plants. The easiest source of water was rain, so it was important that the rains came regularly.

They also knew that various plants produced seeds and that these seeds produced more of the same kind of plants. They observed that animals and birds produced offspring that grew into the same kind of animals as their parents. They knew that, in a way similar to animals, men and women produced children. Because they were human and because they knew all of this, they believed that God had given human beings a special place in the world. They further believed that God had made everything that existed by simply "saying" that all things were to be. They understood speech as the distinctive ability of God and of humans.

After God created everything else, he made a man and a woman. According to the story, God made the man first and then made the woman from a part of the man. The man and the woman were special because God made them in his image and likeness. Nothing else God created was so distinguished.

When man was complete, he placed him and woman in a garden and told them to take care of it. He meant that they should cultivate the garden and enjoy everything the garden produced. Evidently, there were many fruit trees and other good things to eat growing in the garden.

God's whole creation was very pleasant. When he looked at it, he saw that it was very good—just as he had intended it to be. He managed to finish it all in six days. Because it had been such a tremendous task, he spent the seventh day resting. This is how the idea developed that humans should rest every seventh day—just as God rested.

There was only one small stipulation that God placed on the man and woman. There were two trees in the garden that deserved special attention: the tree of life in the middle of the garden and the tree of the knowledge of good and evil. God told the man and woman not to eat any fruit from the tree of the knowledge of good and evil. He warned them that if they did eat the fruit, they would die.

Now the story of the Bible takes an unexpected turn. In the garden, there was a talking snake. One day, the snake engaged the woman in a debate over God's instruction. The woman explained that if they ate the fruit, they would die. The snake contradicted God, telling the woman that what would really happen was that she and the man would become just like God if they ate the fruit.

The woman considered the tree again. The fruit appeared to be the most luscious in the garden. She decided that anything that looked that good must have great worth. So, she took some of the fruit, ate it, and shared it with the man.

The man and woman then looked at each other and realized they were naked. This hadn't bothered them before, but now they were embarrassed. They decided to sew fig leaves—the scratchiest leaves known—together to make coverings for themselves.

As the afternoon breeze began, they heard God walking in the garden. They were afraid and hid. They hadn't been afraid before, but now they knew they didn't have the proper clothes to meet God. God couldn't find their hiding place, so he called out to them. Instead of keeping quiet, the man immediately spoke up to explain that he had heard God coming and hid because he was naked. "Who told you you were naked?" God asked. "Have you eaten from the tree I told you not to eat from?"

The man blamed the woman for giving him the fruit. The woman, probably vowing under her breath to get even with the man as soon as possible, said to God, "The serpent tricked me and I ate." The serpent, evidently having developed laryngitis, said not a word.

God made the serpent crawl on his belly and made the woman hate the serpent. He then made it painful for the woman to bear children. Finally, God told the man that he would continue to work for his food by farming and by raising livestock. But the earth would not be as cooperative as it had been and the man's work would not be nearly as productive.

God then noted that the man and woman might be able to eat the fruit of the tree of life and live forever. To prevent that, God drove the man and woman out of the garden and assigned a heavenly being to guard the entrance so that they could not return.

The story of the first man and woman is a parable of the human condition. Human beings have used their minds to acquire an incredible amount of knowledge, and with that knowledge, they have created both good and evil. The capacity of human beings to behave inhumanely seems infinite. As a result, our knowledge has created a vast chasm between God and us.

After their banishment from the garden, their situation rushed rapidly downhill. Adam and Eve—as they are now named—had two sons, Cain and Abel. Cain was a farmer and Abel a shepherd. Both made an offering to God. Cain offered some of his grain and Abel offered some of his sheep. God accepted Abel's offering but ignored Cain's. Cain became jealous and angry. He killed Abel and then denied it when God asked him. Cain's real problem was with God, but he couldn't figure out a way to kill God so he took it out on Abel. God punished Cain by making him a wanderer over the earth, but marked him so that no one would harm him.

This is a confusing story—even for Christians very schooled in the teachings of the Bible. No one knows why God refused Cain's offering and accepted Abel's. That is just the way it was.

Nevertheless, the killing of one's brother caused the human situation to deteriorate even further. Things became so bad among humans that God concluded he had made a mistake and decided to wipe them out. He planned to do it by flood. But one man attracted God's attention. His name was Noah. Because God favored Noah, he decided to make an exception of him and save him from the worldwide flood. God told Noah to build a boat and provided him with detailed instructions. When the time for the flood came, God told Noah to take his wife and three sons—Shem, Ham and Japheth, along with their wives—into the boat. Noah also took a pair, male and female, of every creature that lived on the earth. After Noah had completed this task, the rain came and flooded the whole earth, destroying all of humanity and the land animals.

It rained for a long time and then stopped. Eventually, the water dried up and the mountaintops began to appear. Finally, it was dry enough so that Noah, his family, and all the animals could leave the boat. Noah made an altar and offered sacrifices to God.

Shortly after that, Noah planted a vineyard and made wine from the crop. He got drunk and lay naked in his tent. This was not an appropriate thing to do. One of his sons, Ham, saw him naked. The other two sons covered Noah without looking at him. When he woke up, Noah cursed Ham's son, Canaan, which seems unfair since Canaan had no part in what his father had done.

The story of a great flood is not unique to the Bible. There were at least four other stories of a flood, like the one in the Bible, in the literature of the societies around ancient Israel. They are similar enough so that it is obvious that someone was borrowing from whichever one was written first. The difference between the biblical story and the others is that the others make a divine figure of their hero and there is more than one god in each story. In the Bible, Noah is very much human. He is not morally perfect, nor does human sinfulness stop after the flood. Noah eventually dies, admittedly at a ripe old age, but he is clearly mortal. The Bible has only one God.

The story of the flood shows that God is in charge of the world and is not going to let it spin out of control. There was a danger, before the flood, that humanity would become so depraved that God would have no chance to make it anything like what he intended it to be. So he brought a dramatic end to the situation and started again with what he hoped would be a world more receptive to his plan.

Another story about the whole earth follows the story of Noah and the ark. It is a story about the Tower of Babel. It seems that all the people of the earth gathered in the plain between the Tigris and Euphrates Rivers. There, they built a city called "Babel" (Babylon in English). In the middle of the city, they built a tower reaching up to heaven so that they could ascend to the level of God. They could do this because, at that time, there was only one language and it had very few words. They could all understand one another very well. But God was distressed that the people aspired to be on his level. So he confused them by causing them to speak many different languages. Because they could not understand each other, they stopped building the tower and scattered from the plain over the surface of the earth.

The story explains why there are many languages and why people cannot understand each other. After the experience at Babel, human beings are not only alienated from God, but also alienated from one another. From God's point of view, that is the way the world is now and will remain until humanity accepts his plan for changing those two basic relationships.

At the end of the Babel story, God's creation of the earth is complete. Genesis 12 begins with God's call to Abraham. Though we have no literary mention of Abram/Abraham outside the Bible, archaeologists have shown that he lived in our historical world around 2000 BCE (Before the Common Era, 2000 years before the birth of Jesus Christ). We have discovered the place from which he came and we know the places where he went.

Abraham came from Ur, a city located near the mouth of the Euphrates River. He moved north along the Euphrates to the city of Haran and settled there. One day, he heard God tell him to go out on his own to a place that God would show him. God promised Abraham that he would be the father of a great and numerous people and that he would possess the land. At the age of 75, he took Sarah, his wife, and Lot, his nephew, and left for the promised land. They came to Canaan (modern day Palestine) and Abraham built an altar at Bethel and worshiped the Lord. At that time, Abraham and Sarah had no children.

When there was a famine in Canaan, Abraham went to Egypt with Sarah and Lot. Because Sarah was beautiful, Abraham feared Pharaoh, the ruler of Egypt, would kill him in order to marry Sarah. Abraham told Sarah to say she was his sister. Pharaoh took her as a wife and subsequently contracted a disease. So he sent Abraham, Sarah and Lot out of Egypt with enough food to survive the famine.

After they returned to Canaan, Abraham and Lot found they had too much livestock for the section of land they were sharing. Abraham offered Lot his choice of the plain around Jericho, Sodom and Gomorrah, a territory well watered and lush, or the hill country. Lot chose Sodom and Abraham went to live in the hill country near Hebron.

Sometime later, a coalition of kings from the east attacked Sodom and captured Lot. Abraham gathered his men and went after the kings' army, defeated them and rescued Lot. Abraham gave a tenth of all that he had captured from the kings to the Lord.

Now well advanced in years and still childless, Sarah decided to take action. She gave her servant, Hagar, to Abraham and told him to use her as a surrogate mother for a child that would legally belong to Sarah and Abraham. Perhaps in this way God's promise would be fulfilled. Everything worked according to plan, except that Hagar became contemptuous of her mistress. Infuriated, Sarah drove Hagar away. God found Hagar in the desert and told her to go back to Sarah and behave herself. Hagar had a son, Ishmael, whom Abraham and Sarah adopted.

God came to visit Abraham again near Hebron where he lived with Sarah. This time, he brought two angels with him. God told Abraham that Sarah would become pregnant and bear a son. Overhearing, Sarah laughed at God. So God said the boy's name would be Isaac, which means "laughter."

Sarah had a son as God had promised and they named him Isaac. When Sarah weaned Isaac, she became distressed that Hagar and Ishmael were still with them and that Abraham might love Ishmael more than Isaac. She told Abraham to send Hagar and Ishmael out of the camp again. This time, God agreed with Sarah's plan. Hagar and Ishmael were banished to the desert. God sent an angel to show Hagar where to find water. Ishmael survived and later became the leader of a great nation.

When Isaac was a young teenager, God told Abraham that he should take Isaac to the top of a local mountain and offer him as a sacrifice. The Bible doesn't tell us how Abraham felt about this. Abraham made all the preparations to kill Isaac on top of the mountain. Just as he was about to plunge the knife into Isaac, God spoke from heaven and stopped him. Evidently, God only wanted to see how far Abraham would go in obeying an irrational command. God repeated his promise to grant Abraham land and a large number of descendants.

After the incident with Isaac, the Bible's account of Abraham comes swiftly to an end. Sarah dies and Abraham contracts with some of the people of the land to buy a field with a cave so that he can bury Sarah. Rather than have Isaac marry one of the foreigners among whom they were living, he sends a servant back to Haran to find a wife for Isaac among his relatives there. The servant finds Rebekah and brings her back to Beersheba where Isaac lived. Isaac marries Rebekah.

Abraham died at the age of 175. Isaac and Ishmael buried him in the cave with Sarah. It was the only portion of the land that belonged to him and Isaac was the only descendant of Sarah and Abraham. This was the state of God's promise of numerous descendants and a great territory upon Abraham's death.

Isaac and Rebekah had twin sons. Isaac favored the older son, Esau, and Rebekah was partial to the younger son, Jacob. Being the older of the two, if only by minutes, Esau was entitled to the birthright and the larger portion of the inheritance. Through his own foolish behavior and some trickery by his mother and brother, Jacob received Esau's birthright. Jacob had to leave home and live with his uncle, Laban, for many years because Esau wanted to kill him over the issue of the birthright. Laban, Rebekah's brother, was from the same region as Abraham.

During the time that Jacob lived with Laban, he married both of Laban's daughters, Leah and Rachel. Jacob had wanted to marry only Rachel, but Laban tricked him into marrying Leah first. Both Leah and Rachel had handmaids, Zilpah and Bilhah. Jacob proceeded to have children by all four of these women, creating a blended family. By Leah, he had Reuben, Simeon, Levi, Judah, Issachar and Zebulon. By Rachel, he had Joseph and Benjamin. By Zilpah, he had Gad and Asher. By Bilhah, he had Dan and Naphtali. Later in the story, Jacob received a new name, Israel. The name means, "He who strives with God." Israel became the name for the nation that had twelve tribes named after the sons of Jacob.

Eventually, Jacob decided he wanted to take his wives, children and all the flocks and herds that he had acquired while working for Laban, and return to the land of Canaan. Laban did not want to let him go, but Jacob insisted and they separated as bitter enemies.

Jacob was very concerned about the reception that he would receive from Esau. To ameliorate his brother's anger, he sent some of his servants ahead of him with gifts of sheep and cattle for Esau, who was meeting him with 400 men. As it turned out, Esau was very gracious to Jacob and forgave him for cheating him out of his birthright. Though the two of them were never close friends, they managed to live in peace.

Several years passed and Jacob's twelve sons grew older. They established families of their own and the number of people related to Jacob/Israel also grew. Because Joseph and Benjamin were the sons of Jacob's favorite wife, he was partial to them, especially to Joseph. He gave Joseph a very beautiful and colorful coat that made him the envy of all his brothers. Joseph, being somewhat spoiled, had two dreams that he interpreted to mean that his brothers, and even his mother and father, would at some time bow down to him. His brothers resented his attitude and planned to get rid of him. One day, when Joseph came to find his brothers, they seized him, took his coat from him and sold him to a passing caravan going to Egypt. The brothers tore Joseph's beautiful coat and smeared it with goat's blood. They showed it to Jacob and claimed that a wild beast had killed Joseph.

When the caravan arrived in Egypt, Joseph was sold to an officer of Pharaoh's court. Joseph proved so trustworthy that he was allowed to manage the officer's business and household dealings. But the officer's wife fell in love with Joseph and tried to seduce him. When he ran away from her, she told her husband that Joseph had tried to rape her. The officer had Joseph thrown into prison.

After Joseph had been in prison for several years, Pharaoh had a troubling dream. None of his court could interpret its meaning. Then one of them remembered that Joseph had interpreted a dream for him while in prison. Pharaoh sent for Joseph and told him about his dream. Joseph told the Pharaoh that it meant there would be seven years of excellent harvests in Egypt followed by seven years of terrible harvests. Pharaoh was impressed and decided to put Joseph in charge of Egypt's agriculture. Joseph made the Egyptians store a large amount of the grain produced during the seven good years so that there would be enough food during the years of poor harvests. In ruling Egypt, he became second only to Pharaoh.

When the seven years of poor harvests came, Egypt was ready. The poor crops, however, were not limited to Egypt. There was famine in other parts of the world as well, including Canaan, where Joseph's father, brothers and their families lived. The famine became so severe that Jacob sent ten of his sons to Egypt to buy grain. He kept Joseph's brother, Benjamin, at home because, with Joseph gone, Benjamin was now Jacob's favorite son.

When the brothers arrived in Egypt, they were taken to see Joseph. He recognized them, but they did not recognize him. Joseph made demands of his brothers, including bringing Benjamin with them when they next traveled to Egypt. He also played tricks on them as tests to see if their attitude had changed in the years since they had sold him as a slave. Their reactions to the tests convinced Joseph that they had indeed changed. He told them who he was and then asked about his father.

Joseph then sent his brothers home with enough wagons and supplies to bring his father and all their families back to Egypt to settle in the Nile delta where Pharaoh had provided land for them. Thus, all of the people descended from Abraham through Isaac and Jacob came to live in Egypt.

Jacob died in Egypt. Joseph and his brothers returned his

body to Canaan and buried him in the cave with Abraham and Sarah.

After Jacob died, Joseph's brothers were afraid that Joseph would punish them because of what they had done to him. But Joseph reassured them that what had happened was God's way of providing for the survival of all the people of Israel. Though the brothers intended evil for him, God had brought good out of it.

Joseph died in Egypt and his body was embalmed. Before his death, he asked his brothers to take his body to the land of Canaan when God would bring them out of Egypt and lead them there.

2

A LOT OF PEOPLE AND A LAW

After many years had passed, a new Pharaoh ruled in Egypt who did not remember Joseph or the favor that his predecessor had promised Joseph's family. This Pharaoh decided that he wanted to build new cities in Egypt. He needed cheap labor to make the bricks and build the buildings. The number of Israelites in Egypt had increased greatly, so Pharaoh decided to make slaves of them for the work he had planned.

The Egyptians were ruthless taskmasters and treated their Israelite slaves very badly. When the Israelites complained, the Egyptians made their work even more difficult.

Pharaoh decided that the Israelite population was increasing too rapidly. He told the midwives of the Israelites to kill all the male babies. The midwives refused, so Pharaoh commanded that all male infants be thrown into the Nile. A Levite couple had a child and the mother put the baby in a basket and floated him on the river. His older sister, Miriam, saw Pharaoh's daughter pull the basket from the water and take the baby to the palace to care for him. The child was named Moses and his mother went to Pharaoh's daughter and became the baby's nurse.

Moses grew up in Pharaoh's house, but his mother made sure he knew he was an Israelite. One day, when he had become a man, he saw an Egyptian beating some of the Israelites. Moses became angry, killed the Egyptian and hid his body. The next day, several Israelites confronted Moses with what he had done. He decided that if he stayed in Egypt, he would be arrested for murder and executed, so he fled from Egypt to the land of Sinai. There he met a tribal leader named Jethro, became one of his shepherds, and eventually married one of Jethro's daughters.

Moses might well have spent the rest of his life in Sinai (also called "Midian") tending his father-in-law's sheep. But one day, while on Mt. Sinai, a mountain that was so important it was sometimes called the "Mountain of God," Moses saw a burning bush. As Moses turned toward the bush that, though on fire, was not destroyed, God spoke to him. God told Moses that he wanted him to return to Egypt and lead the Israelites out of the land. Moses didn't want to do it. He asked who God was and God told him that his name was "Yahweh" and that he was the God of Abraham, Isaac and Jacob. Moses responded that he could not persuade Pharaoh to let the Israelites go. God showed him two remarkable things he could do to impress the Israelites and Pharaoh. He turned Moses' staff into a snake and then back into a staff. Moses next put his hand in his cloak and it came out leprous; he put it in again and it came out healed. Still, Moses declined, citing his stuttering problem. God told him that he would have Aaron, Moses' brother, go with him to Pharaoh and that Aaron could speak for him.

Reluctantly, Moses went, taking his wife and son with him. When he arrived in Egypt, the Israelites did not receive him enthusiastically. Nevertheless, he and Aaron went to see Pharaoh and demanded that he let the Israelites go. Pharaoh refused, so God sent ten plagues on Egypt. The water of the Nile turned to blood. Fish died, frogs came up on the land and died, gnats and locusts swarmed over Egypt, a horrendous hail storm destroyed the crops, and darkness fell over all the land of Egypt even during the day. All these plagues affected the Egyptians, but did not affect the homes of the Israelites.

Finally, the Lord (another name for "Yahweh" or "God") told Moses that he was going to send a plague on the Egyptians so horrible that Pharaoh would certainly let the Israelites go. Moses and Aaron told Pharaoh that on the following night, the Lord would pass through Egypt and kill all the first-born humans and animals of every kind. Pharaoh still refused to let the Israelites go.

The next night, following instructions from God, all the Israelite families sacrificed a lamb and smeared its blood on the doorposts of their houses. They then ate the lamb and other specially prepared foods. During the hours of darkness, all the Israelites remained inside. The Angel of Death passed over Egypt. Wherever he saw the blood of the lamb, he spared the first-born. In all other houses and barns, the first-born children and animals died. This is the origin of the Hebrew Feast of Passover.

In the morning, Pharaoh sent word that the Israelites could leave Egypt immediately. Moses set out at the head of all the Israelites and they marched toward the Red Sea. Soon after they were gone, however, Pharaoh changed his mind and sent his best troops in chariots to return the Israelites back Egypt. The troops caught up with the Israelites on the shore of the Red Sea. They would have captured them, but the Lord put a pillar of fire between Pharaoh's army and the Israelites.

As the sun rose, Moses lifted his staff over the Red Sea and the water was miraculously divided so that it stood like a wall on each side of a path through the middle. The Israelites marched through on dry ground. Pharaoh's army, seeing that the Israelites were escaping, followed them through the sea. As soon as the Israelites reached the other side, the walls of water collapsed and drowned the entire Egyptian army. The Israelites were now free to continue their journey to the Promised Land, the Land of Canaan.

The Israelites celebrated. Moses and Miriam led them in dancing and singing because they had escaped the Egyptians. God had freed them from many years of slavery. Now they could proceed to the Promised Land. But instead of going directly to the Land of Canaan, Moses led them down the Sinai Peninsula to the Mountain of God, Mount Sinai. On the way, the people became hungry and thirsty. They complained to Moses and Aaron. Moses reported the complaint to God and God made some nearby water sweet to drink by having Moses throw a piece of wood in it. Then God told Moses to tell the people that quail would fly over the camp in the evening and in the morning there would be bread from heaven for them to eat. These things happened as the Lord had said. The people did not know what the "bread" was because it looked like dew on the ground. They called the bread "manna," a word that in Hebrew means, "What is it?" Every morning they gathered enough for every person to eat.

While the Israelites were traveling toward the Mountain of God, they were attacked by the Amalekites. Moses went up on a mountain overlooking the battle, while Joshua, Moses' lieutenant, led the men doing the fighting. When Moses held his hands up, the Israelites won. When he had to lower his hands, the Amalekites won. Finally, Aaron and Hur, who were with Moses on the mountain, held Moses' arms in the air so that the Israelites could decisively defeat the Amalekites. The contending forces were so closely matched that God's power, through Moses' upraised arms, decided the victory.

Moses' father-in-law, Jethro, came into the camp while they were still going toward Mt. Sinai. He saw that Moses was acting as judge for the disputes of all the people with one another. Jethro realized that Moses could not continue to do all the work involved in leading the people if he tried to handle every little controversy by himself. He advised Moses to divide the people into smaller groups and appoint men whose judgment he trusted to handle the conflicts in each group. Then, if a situation beyond the ability of one of the judges arose, he could bring the complaint to Moses for his final opinion.

Three months after they had left Egypt, the people finally arrived at Mt. Sinai. The presence of God appeared on Mt. Sinai as thunder, lightning, a trumpet blast and a thick cloud. God told the people to stand respectfully before the mountain, but that he wanted only Moses and Aaron to come up the mountain to meet him. When Moses met God on Mt. Sinai, God gave him the Torah, the Hebrew word for "Law." The first part of the Torah consisted of Ten Commandments. They are:

1. The Israelites will worship no other God than the Lord who brought them out of Egypt.
2. The people will not make any statue, or idol, to represent God and worship it.
3. They will not speak the name of the Lord casually.
4. They will keep the Sabbath, making every seventh day a day of rest because God rested on the seventh day after creating the earth.
5. Every Israelite shall honor his or her father and mother.
6. They shall not murder.
7. They shall not commit adultery.
8. They shall not steal.
9. They shall not lie, especially when they are serving as witnesses in trials.
10. They shall not enviously desire anything that belongs to someone else.

The Torah included many other laws and directions for the behavior of the people. But these first ten laws had a unique place. The acceptance of the Law made the people a nation under God, a nation that the Lord called "his own special people."

When Moses came down from the mountain, he wrote down all the words of the Lord. The writing was "The Book of the Covenant," the agreement between the Lord and the people of Israel. Moses led the people in an act of worship in which he consecrated them by sprinkling the blood of sacrificed oxen on them and on The Book of the Covenant. The people swore that they would keep the Law by being obedient to the commandments of the Lord.

Moses returned to the top of Mt. Sinai, taking only Joshua with him. The Lord gave him further instructions about the life and worship of the people. In great detail, God described for Moses the construction of a tent, called "the Tabernacle," which was to be the place where the Israelites would gather to worship the Lord. It was to be a very elaborate structure with an altar for making sacrifices of grain and of animals. There would be a very special place in which the two stone tablets of the Torah would be kept. God described a gold-plated box called "The ark of the Covenant" to store the tablets. The Tabernacle and the ark had to be portable so that it could be carried when the Israelites moved from campsite to campsite in the Sinai wilderness.

Along with building of the Tabernacle, God told Moses to ordain Aaron and his sons as priests to conduct the worship services. The priests were to wear special clothing and be set apart because of their special function as leaders of Israel's worship.

Giving all these instructions to Moses took a long time. Moses was on Mt. Sinai for many days and nights. Meanwhile, in the Israelite camp, things were not going well. The people were becoming restless and beginning to think that Moses had died on the mountain. Since they had been told by God not to go near the mountain, there was no way to find out. So they went to Aaron and asked him to make another god for them. Aaron collected all their gold jewelry and melted it in a fire. From the melted gold, Aaron fashioned the image of a calf and told the Israelites to worship the golden calf. The worship degenerated rapidly into a wild, drunken orgy.

God told Moses and Joshua, who had accompanied Moses, to go down from the mountain because the people had gone wild. When Moses saw the scene in the Israelite camp, he became so angry that he threw down the tablets with the Law and broke them in pieces. He took the calf, ground it to powder, poured the powder on the water and made the Israelites drink it. Then he summoned the Levites, the members of his tribe, and sent them throughout the camp to slaughter the leaders of the orgy. They killed about 3,000 people.

The Lord was extremely angry with his people. He threatened to consume all of them and find another people. Moses went back up Mt. Sinai to plead with God to change his mind. Moses was successful and God decided that he would continue to work with the Israelites. He gave Moses tablets to replace the ones he had destroyed.

When Moses returned from the mountain, he gathered the people and told them what the Lord had commanded him to do. He took an offering from all the people and set them to work building the Tabernacle according to the directions God had given him. The work on the Tabernacle took many days. When it was finished, Moses led the people in dedicating the Tabernacle and consecrating the priests who were to serve the Lord in it. It was a great day of celebration, a day in which the people became a nation under God.

The Torah that God gave Moses was extensive. It included many details about the way the people of Israel should worship the Lord and the duties of the priests. There were restrictions about what the Israelites could eat and the way they should relate to family members and others. All of these laws set Israel apart from the other tribes and nations around them. They were forbidden to worship any god other than Yahweh.

After many days in the region of Mt. Sinai, the Israelites broke camp and headed toward Canaan, the Promised Land. As they approached Canaan, Moses sent twelve spies, one man from each tribe, to explore the land. The spies were to determine how many people lived there and how strong their military forces were.

When they returned, the spies reported that the land was good and the fruit and other crops were plentiful. They also said that the towns were strongly fortified and that there were giants in the land who made them feel like grasshoppers. Ten of the spies believed there was no way the Israelites could conquer Canaan. Only Joshua and Caleb insisted the people should trust the Lord and go in and take possession of the land.

The people listened to the ten. They all cried out against the Lord, saying that it would have been better if they had stayed in Egypt rather than face death fighting the inhabitants of Canaan.

The Lord was furious and told Moses that he would kill all of them and make a better people out of the descendants of Moses. Moses pleaded with God to change his mind. God finally relented, but told Moses that all the people, except Joshua and Caleb, would die in the wilderness. Only the sons and daughters of those who left Egypt would enter the Promised Land.

Word that they would die in the wilderness caused so much distress among the Israelites that some of them rebelled against Moses. The leaders of the revolt were Korah, Dathan and

Abiram. Moses and Aaron confronted these groups at the entrance to the Tabernacle. God threatened to destroy the whole people, but Moses pleaded with him to punish only those who had participated in the rebellion.

God told Moses to warn the people to stand away from the tents of Korah, Dathan and Abiram. As soon as Moses had finished speaking, an earthquake opened the ground and the three men and their families were swallowed alive. When the people continued to rebel against Moses, the Lord sent a plague throughout the whole camp and many thousands died. Moses had Aaron offer burning incense to the Lord and the plague was finally stopped.

As the Israelites wandered in the wilderness of Sinai, they came to a place called Kadesh where they camped. Miriam, Moses' sister, died in Kadesh and was buried. After many months, the water ran out. Once again the people complained against Moses, saying that it would have been better to die in Egypt than to die of thirst in the wilderness. Moses spoke to God about the lack of water. The Lord told Moses to take the people, have them stand before a rock outcropping near Kadesh, and strike the rock with his staff. Moses struck the rock and water poured from it. But Moses had not told the people he was acting at God's direction, leaving the impression that it was he who had accomplished this miracle. God, therefore, told Moses that he would also die in the wilderness and that Joshua would lead the people into the Promised Land.

From Kadesh, the Israelites set out toward the plain of Moab that lay on the east bank of the Jordan across from Jericho. While they were traveling toward Moab, two kings, Sihon of the Amorites and Og of Bashan, fought to stop the people from passing through their territory. Under the Lord's guidance, the Israelites defeated both of those kings.

While they were encamped on the plain of Moab, Balak, the

king of Moab, decided that he wanted to destroy the people rather than allow them to take the land of Canaan. But he had heard of the defeat of Sihon and Og and was fearful. Balak enlisted Balaam, a Babylonian diviner, to curse Israel. But the Lord spoke to Balaam so that instead of cursing Israel, he blessed them three times. Balak was furious and sent Balaam back to his home. Because Balaam had blessed Israel, however, Balak also returned home and did not try to defeat Israel.

Finally, the time came for Moses to die. He gathered the people in their camp on the east side of the Jordan and delivered a farewell address, reminding them of the way the Lord had led them through the wilderness. He reviewed the Torah with them, repeating the Ten Commandments almost verbatim. He added a statement that became a creed for Israel: "Hear, O Israel, the Lord is our God, the Lord alone. You shall love the Lord your God with all your heart, and with all your soul, and with all your might." He instructed the people to be diligent in teaching the Torah to their children through all the generations.

He cautioned them further about how they should behave when they had conquered and occupied the Promised Land. He was concerned that the time would come when they would forget the way the Lord had led them and provided for them. They would come to believe that it was by their own strength that they had entered the land, taken the cities, and increased their wealth.

Moses was also worried that the Israelites would worship gods other than Yahweh. He sternly commanded them to guard themselves against bowing before false gods. They were to destroy any person, family or town that worshiped idols or other gods. He told the people that when they entered the Promised Land, the Lord would choose a place where he would set his name. The people were to go to that place and to that place only to worship.

Toward the end of his sermon, Moses challenged the Israelites to set the Law of the Lord in their hearts so that they would keep it always. He offered them the choice of life or death, blessing or curse, good or evil. He pleaded with them to choose life, so that they would live long in the land. He promised that if they kept the Law, they would experience blessings from the Lord all their lives. If they chose another god, they would be cursed and die.

Then Moses told the Israelites that when they had taken the land of Canaan, half of them were to stand on top of Mount Gerizim and half of them on top of Mount Ebal. The two mountains were close together near the city of Shechem. Those on Mount Gerizim would speak blessings over the people and those on Mount Ebal would shout curses. The blessings were for those who faithfully kept the Torah. The curses were for acts that broke a command of Torah.

When he had finished speaking, Moses went to the top of Mount Nebo and looked across the Jordan into the Promised Land. He died and God buried him in Moab. No human knew the place of his grave. He was 120 years old when he died and his sight was clear and his strength still with him.

Joshua then became the leader of the tribes. He sent two men into the Promised Land as spies in order to determine the military strength of the people, especially the people of Jericho. A prostitute of the city hid the spies. In return, they promised her that they would protect her and her family when the Israelites invaded the land.

The spies returned and reported all they had seen to Joshua. He led the people to the edge of the Jordan River. The priests who were carrying the ark of the Covenant went into the river first. When they stepped into the water, the Jordan stopped flowing. The people crossed the river on dry ground. When the last person reached the west bank, the priests came from the middle of the riverbed and the water began to flow again.

The Israelites laid siege to Jericho. Every day they marched around the city, blowing their trumpets. On the seventh day, they marched around the city seven times, blew their trumpets and shouted. The walls of Jericho fell down and the whole city was destroyed. Only the prostitute who had befriended the spies and her family were saved.

After the capture of Jericho, Joshua sent a group of men to attack the small city of Ai and destroy it. But the warriors of Ai defeated the men. Joshua asked the Lord why his army had been defeated and the Lord told him that an Israelite family had taken some of the booty from Jericho for themselves, rather than destroying it as the Lord had instructed. At the direction of the Lord, Joshua held an inquiry and discovered that Achan, of the tribe of Judah, was the guilty man. Joshua brought Achan and his whole family to a valley. The Israelites stoned them to death and burned the bodies. After this, the Israelites successfully defeated Ai.

Then Joshua and the people moved against the kings of Jerusalem, Hebron, Jarmuth, Lachish and Eglon, in the southern part of the land. Again, Joshua and his people were victorious. Joshua had the five kings killed and hung their bodies on trees until the sun went down. The bodies were then thrown into a cave.

Having conquered the cities of southern Canaan, Joshua turned north and defeated a coalition of kings who had allied themselves with Jabin, the king of Hazor. Joshua defeated them, captured Hazor and burned the city to the ground.

By this time, Joshua had grown old. Though a significant portion of the land was in Israelite control, other peoples still ruled much territory. The Lord told Joshua to assign portions of the land to nine tribes and half of the tribe of Manasseh. The tribes of Reuben, Gad and the other half of Manasseh would return to the land assigned to them on the eastern side of the Jordan. Thus, the land was divided among twelve tribes with Ephraim and Manasseh taking the place of Joseph in the tribal list. Joshua did not assign any territory to the tribe of Levi because they were the priests of the Lord. The peoples' offerings to the God of Israel would be Levi's inheritance.

When Joshua had completed the assignment of the tribes to their territories, he gathered all the elders, leaders, judges and officers of Israel to Shechem. There, he made a covenant between the people and Yahweh. He reviewed the history of the people, beginning with Abraham and his family who had worshiped other gods in the land beyond the Euphrates River. He challenged the people to choose whom they would serve, the gods worshiped by their ancestors, the gods of the Canaanites, or Yahweh. He told them that, regardless of their choice, he and his family would serve the Lord. The people promised with an oath that they would be faithful to Yahweh.

Joshua died and the Israelites buried him. The tribes lived side by side with no central government. The only thing that united them was their common allegiance to Yahweh and to his shrine at Shechem.

As the generation of people who had traveled in the wilderness died, their children's faith in God lapsed. They turned to worship the gods of the Canaanite people. Whenever they did this, things went badly for them. They would then remember the Lord and plead with him for help. God would send a powerful person to lead them out of trouble, usually through military victory over their enemies. The powerful person, called a "judge," would summon people from as many of the tribes as would respond in order to fight the battle. When the conflict was over, the people would return to their normal lives and again forget the Lord.

The stories of the Judges are remarkable. Deborah was an Ephraimite who led Israel with the help of Barak, who was from the tribe of Naphtali. She and Barak defeated Sisera, a Canaanite king who threatened the northern part of the land.

Gideon, from the tribe of Manasseh, raised an army to defeat the Midianites when they threatened Israel. God limited the number of men who fought the Midianites with Gideon so that they would know that the victory had been won by the Lord and not by superior military power. Gideon was so successful against the Midianites that his son, Abimelech, attempted to become king of Israel. He was killed in battle and Israel continued without a king.

Jephthah, a man of Gilead, became a judge, defeated the Ammonites, and, because he had made a vow to the Lord, sacrificed his daughter, his only child, as an offering to the Lord.

The last renowned judge of Israel was Samson, from the tribe of Dan. His great physical strength was legendary. He is reported single-handedly to have killed one thousand Philistines. He was eventually captured by the Philistines, blinded, and brought before them in one of their temples. While they were celebrating his capture, Samson pulled down two pillars of the temple, collapsing the building and killing 3,000 Philistines. Samson himself was also killed.

As the time of the Judges came to a close, the Israelite tribes were increasingly threatened by the military power of the Philistines. They lived along the southern coastal plain of Canaan and gave their name to the land, Palestine. The Israelite tribes lived in the hill country. It became ever more clear that they could not survive unless they could defeat the Philistines.

3

SOME KIND OF GOVERNMENT

We do not know how long the Israelites lived under the system of judges. The biblical narrative moves from the story of the tribes to the story of a family and the birth of their child, Samuel. His mother was Hannah and his father Elkanah. Hannah was beyond childbearing age and welcomed Samuel as a gift from the Lord. She dedicated Samuel to God by giving him to the priest, Eli, so he could train Samuel in the Lord's service. Eli was Israel's spiritual leader. He lived in Shiloh, where the ark of the Covenant was housed.

When Samuel became a man, all Israel recognized that God was with him and that he was a trustworthy prophet of the Lord. During that time, the Philistines attacked Israel, defeated its army, and captured the ark of the Covenant. Possession of the ark, however, caused boils on people and a plague of mice among the Philistines. In order to stop the sickness and prevent the mice from destroying the corn, the Philistines sent the ark back to the Israelites on a cart pulled by cows.

After the ark was returned, over twenty years passed and the condition of the tribes had not improved. Samuel gathered the Israelites and berated them for worshiping false gods. The people repented and Samuel led them in battle against the Philistines. Israel was victorious and Samuel set up a stone to commemorate the triumph.

Samuel grew old. His sons did not become the leaders their father had been. The elders of Israel came to Samuel and told him they wanted a king to lead them like the nations around them. Samuel, offended by their request, prayed to the Lord. The Lord told him to listen to the people because it was the Lord whom the people had rejected, not Samuel.

Samuel complied with the desire of the people and the Lord and anointed Saul, whose father was Kish of the tribe of Benjamin. A month or so later, Saul lead the Israelites against the Ammonites, who were attacking the city of Jabesh-Gilead. Saul's army defeated the Ammonites and Saul was thus confirmed as king of Israel.

Several years later, Saul's troops defeated a garrison of the Philistines. The Philistines gathered in force to attack Israel. Samuel had told Saul to wait at Gilgal for seven days so that he could come and offer sacrifices for victory over the Philistines. Samuel's arrival was delayed and, when the seven days had passed, Saul offered the sacrifices himself. Just as he finished the offering, Samuel arrived and confronted him for taking priestly matters into his own hands. He told Saul that because of his presumption, his son would not succeed him.

Despite Samuel's prediction, Saul defeated the Philistines and also defeated the Moabites and Edomites, both enemies of Israel. Samuel told Saul that the Lord wanted him then to attack the Amalekites and punish them for what they did to Israel when the people came out of Egypt. Samuel directed that they all be killed, every man, woman, child and all their animals. But Saul captured Agag, king of the Amalekites, and kept some of the people and some of the animals alive. When Samuel heard of this, he denounced Saul for disobeying the Lord. Samuel killed Agag and then left Saul.

The Lord now directed Samuel to anoint someone to take Saul's place as king. Samuel went to Bethlehem, to the home of a man named Jesse. He was a member of the tribe of Judah. Yahweh told Samuel to anoint the youngest of Jesse's eight sons, David, a boy who was keeping his father's sheep. The anointing had to be kept a secret or Saul would have killed David.

A short time later, Saul became depressed because of the quarrel with Samuel. His depression became so severe that he needed someone to sing soothing songs to comfort him. David was recommended because he had the ability to compose songs for a harp-like instrument called a lyre. He came to Saul's camp and served Saul well.

The Philistines again mustered their army to attack Israel. They camped between Socoh and Azekah, in territory belonging to the tribe of Judah. The Israelite army took up defensive positions against them. Each day, a champion of the Philistines, a ten-foot tall giant named Goliath, came out between the armies to challenge any Israelite to individual combat. Goliath's spear, sword and armor matched his size. No Israelite dared to confront him until David heard his taunt. David volunteered to fight Goliath. He refused Saul's offer of armor, chose five smooth stones from a brook, and, with the stones and a sling went to face the Philistine. He prayed to the Lord and then slung a stone that struck Goliath in the forehead, knocking him to the ground. David took Goliath's own sword and cut off his head. After this great defeat, the Philistine army fled and the Israelites claimed a great victory.

Because of David's accomplishments as a warrior, Saul gave him command of the army. David continued to be successful against the Philistines and all the Israelites began to sing his praises. When Saul heard that the tribes revered David so highly, he became jealous. He feared that David would supplant him and his sons as king. But Saul's son, Jonathan, loved David and became his friend. Michal, Saul's daughter, also loved David and Saul allowed them to marry. This gave David a place within Saul's family and a distant claim to the kingship.

David's success over the Philistines caused a deepening despondency in Saul. He even attempted to kill David one afternoon when David was singing to soothe him. David managed to escape from Saul, but was understandably afraid. Saul tried to trap David at his home, but Michal helped him escape.

Jonathan was deeply distressed with the conflict between his father and David. He went to his father and tried to persuade him to reconcile with David. But Saul became so angry with Jonathan over his friendship with David that he tried to kill his own son. Jonathan left and met David to tell him that it was not safe for David to be in Saul's presence again.

David hid in the wilderness of Judah. Gradually, men whom Saul had angered and who preferred David to Saul began to gather around him. Saul, however, still remained powerful and had a significant following among the people. David had to keep moving, running for his life, because Saul pursued him when the king was not battling the Philistines. One time, though, David had an opportunity to kill Saul because Saul did not realize he was so near. Saul had gone into a cave where David was hiding and did not see him. David's men urged him to kill the king, but David refused. He said that Saul was the Lord's anointed and he would not strike anyone so blessed. He cut off a piece of Saul's robe and, later, showed it to Saul so that he would realize he had been at David's mercy. Saul acknowledged that David was a more righteous man than he.

In time, David's situation became so precarious that he had to ally himself to Achish, the Philistine king of Gath. Achish gave David the town of Ziklag to rule. The town became David's base of operations for the rest of Saul's rule.

The Philistines prepared to fight the Israelites again, this time in the Valley of Jezreel. Saul had doubts about the outcome of the battle, so he consulted a medium at the town of Endor. The medium summoned the ghost of Samuel to come up from Sheol, the place where the Israelites believed the dead went. Samuel's ghost appeared and told Saul that the next day the Philistines would defeat Israel and that Saul and his sons would die.

The Philistines and Israel drew battle lines at Mt. Gilboa in the plain of Jezreel. As Samuel had prophesied, Saul, Jonathan, and several of Saul's other sons died in the battle. The Philistines beheaded Saul and hung his body and the bodies of his sons on the wall of one of their cities. But the men of Jabesh took the bodies down at night and buried them in the town.

David mourned deeply over the death of Saul and Jonathan. When the time of mourning had passed, David moved from Ziklag to Hebron, a city in the tribal land of Judah. There, the elders of Judah made David their king. Abner, Saul's general, made Saul's surviving son, Ishbaal, king over the other tribes of Israel. Civil war broke out between Judah and the other tribes of Israel.

David chose his cousins, Joab, Abishai and Asahel, as the leaders of his army. Abner killed Asahel after one of the battles. Joab and Abishai vowed to revenge Asahel's death by killing Abner.

As the war between Judah and Israel continued, David became stronger and the forces of Israel became weaker. Joab and Abishai managed to kill Abner by treachery. Joab pretended to meet Abner for a conference in the gate of Hebron. When they came close together, Joab stabbed him with a concealed sword. David mourned his death and had him buried in

Hebron. After Abner died, some men, thinking to take advantage of the situation, assassinated Ishbaal and brought his head to David. David recoiled at the sight and had the assassins killed on the spot.

With Abner and Ishbaal dead, the Israelites were unable to continue the conflict with Judah. The leaders of the tribes came to David at Hebron and asked him to be their king. He made a treaty with the others, thus uniting all the tribes under himself.

On becoming king, one of David's first acts was to capture Jerusalem and make it his capital. Until then, Jerusalem had been a Jebusite city, belonging neither to Judah nor to the other tribes of Israel. It became David's city and its population became loyal to him. There, David established his court and garrisoned his standing army. David's rule began in Hebron about 1000 BCE. He ruled there for seven years and from Jerusalem for 33 years.

David decided that the ark of the Covenant should be brought to Jerusalem as a symbol of the religious unity of his rule. He offered sacrifices as the ark was brought along the road and he danced with joy as it came into the tent that he had prepared for it.

Subsequently, David determined to build a temple to house the ark. He asked his prophet, Nathan, about his plan. Prophets were men who spoke God's word to the king and the people. Nathan returned with a message from the Lord that Yahweh would build David's dynasty, but that David's son would build a temple for the ark. God promised David that his covenant love would never leave David's house and that there would always be a ruler of Israel descended from David.

David continued to be successful in battle, decisively defeating the Philistines and other enemy nations around Israel. The treaties he made with some of these kings required that they pay tribute, so the wealth of Israel began to increase.

David was recognized as a "man after God's own heart." But he had a weakness for beautiful women. Standing on the roof of his house one afternoon, he saw one bathing in her courtyard and wondered who she was. One of his servants reported that the woman was Bathsheba, the wife of Uriah, the Hittite, who was in Israel's army and away from Jerusalem fighting. David had an affair with Bathsheba and she became pregnant.

The king sent word to Joab ordering him to send Uriah home so he could sleep with his wife. Uriah came home and reported to David. On his honor as a soldier, he would not sleep with his wife while the army was engaged in combat. Finally, David ordered Uriah back to the front. He sent a secret message to Joab that Uriah should be put in the middle of a battle and then the soldiers around him should retreat so that Uriah would be killed. Joab did as the king commanded and Uriah died. David then took Bathsheba as his wife. She bore David a son.

The Lord was not pleased with David's actions, however. He had Nathan confront David publicly. Even though David repented of his sin before the Lord, nevertheless, Nathan told him that his child would die and that there would be continual conflict in his family.

In spite of David's pleading with God for his life, the child did die. Bathsheba became pregnant again and bore a second son whom David named Solomon.

Throughout the rest of David's reign, there were two major revolts against him. His son, Absolom, led the first uprising, almost succeeding in overthrowing his father as king. In the final battle, however, Absolom's forces were defeated and Absolom himself was killed. In spite of Absolom's treachery, David mourned his death.

The second revolt was led by Sheba, a member of the tribe of Benjamin, Saul's tribe. Though there was much support for this revolt among the northern tribes, Joab and Abishai trapped Sheba in one of the Israelite cities where he was murdered by its inhabitants.

When David came to the end of his life, there was no clear successor to follow him on the throne. David called his priest, Zadok, and several of the leaders of his court. He had Zadok anoint Solomon, his son by Bathsheba, as king. Once this was done, Solomon had a clear path to kingly rule, although he had to have Adonijah, another son of David who aspired to the throne, and Joab, who supported Adonijah, killed.

With his throne secure, Solomon established a kingdom and a court as opulent as any in the ancient Middle East. He brought cedar from Lebanon and hired Tyrian architects to build a temple for the ark and then to build a palace for himself three times larger than the temple. He dedicated the temple, which it had taken seven years to build, with great celebration and many sacrifices and prayers.

Solomon divided his kingdom into twelve districts, roughly corresponding to the old tribal boundary lines. Each district had to supply Solomon's court with its finances and supplies for one month a year. Solomon also conscripted men from the Israelite tribes to work on his building projects. Because David's kingdom had extended across the caravan routes between Egypt and Babylon, the taxes from the traders that passed along the routes were very large. This added to Solomon's wealth and his renown throughout the Middle East.

Solomon had a large number of wives, many of whom he married in order to establish a treaty relationship with their kingly fathers. Toward the end of his life, he began to worship the foreign gods of his wives, thus earning the Yahweh's condemnation.

By the time he died in 922 BCE, Solomon was hated by many of the Israelites, especially the northern tribes who had never been very fond of David either. The elders of the northern tribes came to meet Solomon's son, Rehoboam, and asked him if he planned to continue the practices of his father. Rehoboam thought about it for three days and then responded that he intended to be far more severe than his father. The northern tribes refused to continue under his rule and anointed Jeroboam, the son of Nebat, as their king. Rehoboam was left with only Judah and Benjamin under his authority.

The northern tribes kept the name Israel and the southern tribes were known as Judah. Jeroboam soon realized that the people of his kingdom, Israel, were accustomed to traveling to Jerusalem to worship Yahweh. If they continued to do this, he thought, it would not be long before they would want to reunite with Judah and establish the nation as a unified whole once more. In order to prevent that, he built temples at Bethel on the southern border of Israel's territory and at Dan on the northern border. Jeroboam's people then went to these temples rather than to Jerusalem. The historical books of the Bible favor the temple at Jerusalem and accuse the temples at Bethel and Dan of allowing the worship of other gods than Yahweh, especially the Canaanite god, Baal. The books also accuse Jeroboam of leading Israel to sin.

The two kingdoms continued to exist side by side for the next 200 years, sometimes at war and sometimes peaceably. They were occasionally invaded by Egypt or by Assyria, the empire that dominated the land between the Tigris and the Euphrates in that era. Neither was controlled for very long by any foreign power. Occasionally, they fought together against a common enemy.

Israel, the northern kingdom, was economically and strategically far more important than Judah. The rule of the northern kingdom tended to be decided by revolt against a king or by bloody coup after the king died. The capital was in two other cities before it was moved to the town of Samaria, a city built by Omri, one of Israel's ablest kings, around 880 BCE. The northern king, upon whom a large portion of the biblical record focuses, was a son of Omri named Ahab.

The southern kingdom, Judah, was ruled continuously from Jerusalem. The tradition of Davidic rule was strong in Judah and the king was always a descendant of David. The nation never loomed large on the international stage.

All of the people tended to look back to the united rule of the twelve tribes under David and Solomon as the golden age of Israel. Of the two, David was seen as the ideal king and Solomon's place was accorded him because he built the temple.

The historical books of the Bible have only one standard of judgment by which they evaluate the kings of Israel and Judah: a king is considered a good king if he protects the purity of Israel's worship life and works to centralize the worship of all people in the temple at Jerusalem, closing the outlying shrines. The outlying shrines were seen as places where foreign gods were worshiped and the people went astray.

Since the northern kings did not support the Jerusalem temple, they were judged as unworthy. Only two of the kings of Judah, Hezekiah and Josiah, were praised because they attempted religious reforms that shut down the outlying shrines and concentrated worship life in the temple.

Hezekiah ruled from 715 – 687 BCE (years before Christ's birth decline toward zero). His rule began just seven years after the Assyrians under Sargon II had destroyed the northern kingdom. They had besieged Samaria for two years before it finally surrendered. The Assyrians razed the city and forced most of the leaders of Israel into exile, scattering them throughout the cities of the empire. They then brought foreign people into the territory of the northern kingdom and settled them there. The northern kingdom became known as the "ten lost tribes of Israel," because none of them ever constituted itself again as a political entity.

In 705 BCE, Hezekiah withheld tribute from the Assyrian overlords. In 701 BCE, the Assyrian king, Sennacherib, invaded Judah and besieged Jerusalem. The Lord sent a plague against the Assyrian army and the siege was lifted. Sennacherib returned to Nineveh, the Assyrian capital, and never attacked Jerusalem again. The Judeans, all that was left of Israel, saw their deliverance from the Assyrians as a sign that Yahweh would never allow the city to fall.

From 697 – 640 BCE, the Assyrians were dominant in the Middle East and Judah was nothing more than a province of their Empire. In 640 BCE, Josiah, a great-grandson of Hezekiah, came to the throne of Judah. He was eight years old.

Beginning in 630 BCE, the Assyrian Empire began to collapse. By 626 BCE, the Chaldeans, under king Nabopolassar, had seized Babylon and Assyrian power was in rapid decline. Josiah began a religious reform that climaxed in 622 BCE when, during the renovation of the Temple, a Book of the Law of God was found. It was a portion of Deuteronomy, emphasizing the importance of centralizing worship in Jerusalem. Josiah proceeded to close the outlying shrines and bring the priests and Levites into Jerusalem. The Bible praises him as the greatest king since David.

Josiah's reign did not last long, however. The international situation was changing rapidly. In 612 BCE, Nineveh, the capital of the Assyrian Empire, fell to the Chaldeans under Nabopolassar. In 609 BCE, Pharaoh Necho II of Egypt marched north through Palestine to reinforce the remnants of the Assyrian army fighting with the Chaldeans. Josiah met him at Megiddo. Josiah was killed, either in battle or by a treacherous assassination at Necho's hands. Two months later when Necho returned from fighting with the Assyrians against Nabopolassar, he placed Josiah's son, Jehoiakim, on the throne of Judah. Jehoiakim reversed his father's policies and religious reform came to an end.

Nabopolassar died in 605 BCE. That same year, his son, Nebuchadnezzar, decisively defeated the Assyrians and Egyptians at Carchemish and assumed control of the Middle East. He established a new Babylonian Empire, with its capital at Babylon. Judah was, once more, a vassal territory.

In 598 BCE, Jehoiakim revolted against Babylon. Reacting swiftly, Nebuchadnezzar besieged Jerusalem. Jehoiakim died and his son, Jehoiachin, surrendered the city to the Babylonians. Nebuchadnezzar took Jehoiachin and 3,000 leaders of the country into captivity and settled them near Babylon. He placed Zedekiah, Jehoiachin's uncle, on the throne.

Zedekiah revolted against the Babylonians in 588 BCE. Nebuchadnezzar returned to Judah (from this time on called "Judea") and, after a siege of two years, broke through the walls of Jerusalem and totally destroyed the city. A thousand more people were taken to Babylon to join the original group of captives. Jerusalem lay in ruins without any significant population from 586 – 538 BCE. This period is known as The Exile and marks a climactic break in the history of Israel. The monarchy of David had come to an end. The Temple had been destroyed. The traditional political and religious life of Israel was over. The exiles, now known as Jews (from "Judeans"), gathered their sacred writings and became the people of the Torah.

Nebuchadnezzar ruled the Middle East until his death in 562 BCE. His empire rapidly disintegrated. In 539 BCE, Babylon fell to the Persians under Cyrus. Cyrus' attitude toward vassal people in his empire was very different from Nebuchadnezzar's. He issued an edict allowing the Jewish exiles to return to Jerusalem and reestablish the nation. Enough of them returned over the next 23 years to establish a viable economic and religious community among the ruins of the city. In 515 BCE, under the leadership of Zerubbabel, they completed the rebuilding of the Temple. This second Temple was much less impressive than the first. The younger people rejoiced when it was dedicated, but the older ones, who remembered the glory of Solomon's Temple, wept.

Around 450 BCE, a governor named Nehemiah, led the people in rebuilding the walls of Jerusalem. A short time later, Ezra, a scribe of the law of God, came to Jerusalem from Babylon, bringing a copy of Torah. He assembled all the people and read the law to them. Ezra then instructed the men to divorce their foreign wives and separate themselves from the children born to those wives. From that time on, Jewish men would marry only Jewish women and the law would be strictly observed.

At this point, the historical record of our Old Testament ends. From other writings, some of them called "The Apocrypha," we know more of the history from 400 BCE until the birth of Jesus Christ.

The Persian Empire ruled the Middle East until the rise of the Greeks under the Macedonian king, Alexander the Great. Alexander defeated Darius II of Persia at Issus in 333 BCE. After the battle, he proceeded to conquer Palestine and Egypt. He then turned east, crossed the Euphrates and the Tigris Rivers, and met Darius, with the last of his armies, at Gaugamela in 331 BCE. The Persians were routed and his own men later murdered Darius. Alexander controlled the whole Persian Empire. He proceeded east with his army and crossed into India, heading for what he believed was the end of the earth. His army finally revolted and he returned to Babylon where he died in June, 323 BCE, at the age of 32.

Alexander left no heirs. His generals fought over the territory that he had conquered in his brief life. Ptolemy became ruler over Egypt and Palestine in 301 BCE. Seleucus became the ruler of Asia and established his capital at Antioch. The Ptolemies and the Seleucids were at war for much of the next century. During this time, Palestine, including Judea and Jerusalem, remained under Ptolemaic control. Under the influence of Alexander's successors, Greek became the common language of the Mediterranean basin, the Middle East and much of Asia. In 250 BCE, the Old Testament was translated from Hebrew to Greek so that those who did not know Hebrew could read it.

Toward the close of the Third Century (300 – 200 BCE), Antiochus III became king of the Seleucid Empire. In a series of battles, he defeated the Ptolemaic ruler and took control of Palestine. The Jews in Jerusalem welcomed him, helping to provide provisions for his army. In return, he allowed the Jews to live according to their ancestral laws, exempted the priests and scribes from paying taxes, and provided sacrifices for the Temple worship. He also forbade the import of any ritually unclean meat into Jerusalem.

During this time, a new political and military power had arisen in the west – Rome. Antiochus thought that he could defeat the Roman legions and advanced through Asia Minor into Thrace. He was defeated at Thermopylae in Greece in 191 BCE, and again, decisively, at Magnesia in Asia Minor in 190 BCE. In the peace treaty that followed, he gave up all of Asia Minor.

Antiochus III was succeeded by his son, Antiochus IV, who decided to invade Egypt in 170 BCE. He could not complete his conquest of Egypt because he had to return to Jerusalem, where a high priest, Jason, whom Antiochus had dismissed, had tried to capture the city. Antiochus appropriated the Temple treasure in the process of regaining control. He returned to Egypt in 168 BCE. A Roman senator met him there and told him to leave and not come back. Antiochus complied.

Shortly after this, Antiochus came to the conclusion that the majority of Jews would accept Greek culture and religion. He, therefore, issued an edict forbidding traditional Jewish religious observance on pain of death, and commanding the Jews to eat pork, something strictly forbidden by their Law. A representative of Antiochus went to the small town of Modin in 167 BCE, and assembled the citizens of the community. He ordered a sacrifice to Zeus. When a Jew was about to obey, Mattathias, a priest of the Hasmonean family, stepped forward. He killed both the Jew and Antiochus' representative. Then, with his five sons, he raised the standard of revolt. One of his sons, Judas, was nicknamed "Maccabeus," the "fist." He became the military leader of the Maccabean revolt.

The revolt was successful. In 165 BCE, Judas captured Jerusalem and cleansed the Temple. The anniversary of the event became the Festival of Hanukkah. At this festival, Jews remember the miracle of the temple lamp that burned for eight days with oil enough for only one day.

For the next century, the brothers of Judas and their descendants ruled Judea from Jerusalem. In 64 BCE, the Roman ruler, Pompey, came to Damascus and annexed the Seleucid kingdom. He then turned to Judea where he settled a civil war that had broken out among the Hasmoneans. He captured Jerusalem and made Judea a Roman colony.

In the years that followed, civil war broke out in the Roman Empire after the assassination of Julius Caesar in 44 BCE. In 31 BCE, Octavian was victorious in the battle of Actium and established himself as Emperor. He took the throne name Caesar Augustus. He confirmed Herod, an Idumean, as king of Judea and added Gaza and several coastal cities to his territory. Herod married Mariamne, a Hasmonean descendant, to establish the legitimacy of his claim to the throne. He is known in history as "Herod the Great" and was the ruler of Judea when Jesus Christ was born.

4

THE GOVERNMENT'S CRITICS

A considerable portion of the Old Testament is filled with the stories and writings of a group of men known as "prophets." They are the critics of the kings of both Israel and Judah. They saw themselves as the spokesmen of the Lord, pronouncing God's judgment against both kings and people. When the judgment occurred, several of them spoke of God's redemption and restoration.

Though the historical period of the prophets coincides with the kingdoms of Israel and Judah, their precepts and insights are so important that they require their own place in history. The work of the prophets began with David's rule and came to a close with the completion of Zerubbabel's temple (1000–515 BCE).

The prophet Nathan, you recall, reported God's word to David about his proposal to build the Temple. He later denounced David for his affair with Bathsheba, thereby establishing the prophet's right to hold the king accountable to the Law. Nathan's final act was to anoint Solomon king of Israel.

After Solomon's death, the first significant prophet was

Elijah. His name means, "My God is Yahweh!" He is recognized as the "father" of the prophets. He appears as a mature man and speaks to the king of the northern tribes, Ahab, who ruled from 869–850 BCE. The main problem Elijah confronted was the Israelites' worship of the Canaanite god, Baal. Ahab had married a Sidonian princess named Jezebel. Ahab's father, Omri, arranged the marriage to seal an alliance between Sidon and Israel. Ahab brought Jezebel to Samaria and built a chapel there for the worship of Baal. According to the customs of the time, this was an acceptable thing to do.

Jezebel was an enthusiast for her god, bringing 450 prophets of Baal to Samaria with her. She then proceeded to suppress the worship of Yahweh and persecute his prophets. At this moment, Elijah appeared and announced that there would be no more rain in Israel until God spoke again through him.

Three years later, with a severe famine in the land because of the drought, Elijah met Ahab and denounced him for allowing the worship of Baal. He then summoned all of Israel to a contest on Mt. Carmel, an ancient center for the worship of Baal. He and the prophets of Baal would prepare bulls for sacrifice and whichever deity sent fire, either Baal or Yahweh, would be recognized as God.

When the day came, Elijah permitted the prophets of Baal to go first. They prepared their bull and danced around the altar, screaming out to their god. When no answer came, they gashed themselves and bled on the sacrifice. Elijah mocked them, suggesting that Baal was either asleep or relieving himself. Finally, they gave up.

Elijah then repaired Yahweh's altar, which had been torn down. He prepared the bull, set the wood for fire, doused the wood and the altar three times with water, and prayed a simple prayer. Immediately, fire came from heaven, consuming the wood, the bull, and the altar. The Israelites shouted, "Yahweh is God! Yahweh is God!" At Elijah's direction, they seized the 450 prophets of Baal and killed them all. Shortly afterward, the downpour began.

When Jezebel heard what had happened, she sent word to Elijah that she would deal with him the same way he dealt with her prophets. Elijah was afraid, and he fled south to Mt. Horeb, the Mountain of God. He hid in a cave while a great earthquake shook the mountain. A tremendous wind blew across the cave's mouth and fire burned from the summit of the mountain. Finally, the Lord, who was not in the earthquake, wind or fire, spoke in the sound of silence. Yahweh challenged Elijah by asking, "What are you doing here, Elijah?" Elijah recounted all that Jezebel had done in persecuting Yahweh's prophets and said that he felt he was the only believer left. The Lord assured him that there were still 7,000 men in Israel who were faithful to him and that Elijah should return and anoint Jehu king of Israel. Jehu was a high-ranking officer in the Israelite army, a commoner not descended from any king.

Elijah did as God instructed. Ahab died in battle and his son succeeded him. After Ahab's death, Elijah was taken to heaven in a fiery chariot from the bank of the Jordan River. Elisha became prophet in his place. Later, Jehu raised the standard of revolt and killed Jezebel and all of Ahab's children.

Jehu's dynasty lasted to the fifth generation. His great-grandson, Jeroboam II, ruled Israel from 786–746 BCE. In Judah, King Uzziah (783–742 BCE) was on the throne. These two kings ruled in a time of peace and prosperity that was unequalled since the time of Solomon. The wealth of the rich people in Israel grew to unheard of levels. At the same time, the situation of the peasants, the poor people of the land, became more and more desperate.

The prophet Amos addressed this state of affairs. He spoke God's word to Israel, the northern kingdom, some time around 755 BCE. Amos had come from Judah, but he prophesied in Jeroboam's temple at Bethel. He was the first of the "classical prophets," those who have books of sayings named for them.

Amos was unsparing in his condemnation of the injustices under which the poor suffered. Speaking to the wealthy, he said, "Woe to you who sell the righteous for silver, the needy for a pair of shoes, who trample the head of the poor into the dust of the earth." He was speaking of the court system in which bribes were freely given to judges by the rich to defraud the peasants of their holdings, making them nothing but serfs on their land. He condemned the sexual immorality of the men of Israel. He thundered against the wives of the wealthy, whom he called "cows of Bashan," for their excess luxury and their indifference to the poor. In the name of the Lord, he roared against their worship, calling it an insult to the Lord's ears and blatant hypocrisy. "Take away the noise of your songs; I will not listen to the melody of your harps. But let justice roll down like waters, and righteousness like an everflowing stream."

One of the priests at Bethel, Amaziah, told Amos to go back to Judah and prophesy. Amos denounced Amaziah and denied being a "prophet," scorning the paid "prophets" of the king. He pictured himself as a shepherd whom God had called to speak. He told the Israelites that God had measured them against a plumb line of righteousness and that they had failed the test. They would go into exile.

A second prophet, Hosea, was a close contemporary of Amos. He also spoke against the northern kingdom just after

Jeroboam's death. Hosea was distressed by the lack of the "knowledge of God" among the people. He accused them of "swearing, lying, murder, stealing and adultery," all actions condemned by the Ten Commandments. He railed against the priests for their failure to teach the precepts of the Torah.

Hosea married a woman who deserted him to become a prostitute. He went after her and brought her back, punishing her by prohibiting her from intercourse. Hosea saw in his own experience a parallel to God's faithful love of Israel in spite of Israel's waywardness.

Hosea pictures Israel, which he sometimes refers to as Ephraim, as a child whom God called out of Egypt, to whom God bound himself with cords of love and devotion. But the more God bound himself to Israel, the more she strayed from him. Then, in a heart-rending passage, he hears God's inner struggle, torn between his justice and his loving tenderness: "How can I give you up, Ephraim? How can I hand you over, O Israel? . . . My heart recoils within me: my compassion grows warm and tender. I will not execute my fierce anger; I will not again destroy Ephraim; for I am God and no mortal, the Holy One in your midst, and I will not come in wrath."

Hosea spoke mostly of judgment coming upon Israel. But he also prophesied that in the future God would abolish war and allow Israel to live in safety. Israel would be God's wife in faithfulness and steadfast love. The earth would again be fruitful and the time of punishment would be past. Israel would be God's people again. He would comfort them and they would say, "You are my God."

But it didn't happen this way. The northern kingdom was destroyed by the Assyrians in 722 BCE and the people were exiled, scattered among the towns of the Assyrian Empire.

Judah alone was left.

In the period just before and after the destruction of Samaria, the prophet Micah spoke in Judah about both Samaria and Jerusalem. Micah was from a small town in Judah. He had a deep suspicion about cities, particularly Samaria and Jerusalem. He saw them as hotbeds of sin and intrigue. He witnessed the destruction of Samaria and prophesied that Jerusalem would "become a heap of ruins and the mountain of the house a wooded height." (He was referring to the Temple.)

But Micah, like Hosea, looked beyond the Lord's judgment to see a vision of restoration. He pictured a time when the Lord's house would be raised up above the hills and the people of all nations would come streaming into it. He glimpsed God's universal reign with "Torah going forth from Zion, and the word of the Lord from Jerusalem." He saw God judging among many nations, so that they would "beat their swords into plowshares, and their spears into pruning hooks: nation shall not lift up sword against nation, neither shall they learn war any more."

Being a man of the village, Micah saw a new leader for the nation coming from a Judean village. The town was Bethlehem, the hometown of David, Israel's great king. Micah told of a leader like David who would be a shepherd to his people and would make them secure. He would be renowned as an international leader, a man of peace.

As Amos had before him, Micah expressed strong doubts about the religious system of sacrifices. He saw the Lord involved in a controversy with his people. God reminded the people of what he had done for them in the wilderness after bringing them out of Egypt. Then, Micah wondered aloud how he should come before Yahweh. Would Yahweh be pleased with the sacrifice of calves, rams or rivers of oil?

Should he sacrifice his son for the sins of his soul? Then the answer comes: "He has told you, O mortal, what is good; and what does the Lord require of you but to do justice, and to love kindness, and to walk humbly with your God?" It is the finest summary of faith under Yahweh that the Bible contains.

In the same period as Micah, during the reigns of Ahaz (736–715 BCE) and Hezekiah (715–687 BCE), the prophet Isaiah spoke in Jerusalem. Unlike Micah, Isaiah was a man of the city. From what we learn of him in the book that bears his name, he had easy access to the king and was probably part of the Jerusalem aristocracy. In the year that king Uzziah died (742 BCE), Isaiah had a vision of God while he was worshiping in the Temple. He saw Seraphim, angelic beings, flying around the throne of God and crying, "Holy, holy, holy is the Lord of hosts; the whole earth is full of his glory." Brought to his knees by the vision, Isaiah cried out that he was lost and that his speech was impure in God's hearing. But God acted to purify his speech. Then Isaiah heard God asking who would go for him. Isaiah immediately responded, "Send me!" The Lord gave him a message of judgment to take to the people of Israel and Judah – that the land would be destroyed and the inhabitants killed in war.

In 734 BCE, Isaiah attempted to persuade the Judean king, Ahaz, not to join a coalition with Rezin, king of Damascus, and Pekah, king of Israel in Samaria, against the Assyrians under king Tiglath-pileser. Since Rezin and Pekah were threatening to attack Judah if Ahaz did not agree to become their ally, Isaiah also cautioned Ahaz not to ask for help from Tiglath-pileser. During their encounter, Isaiah told Ahaz that God would give him a sign. A young woman would bear a son and he would be named Immanuel, which means "God with us."

Ahaz did not take Isaiah's advice. He made an alliance with Tiglath-pileser and the Assyrians conquered Damascus in 732 BCE. In Samaria, Hoshea, the last king of Israel, the northern kingdom, replaced Pekah. Samaria and Israel fell to the Assyrians in 722 BCE.

In many of the things that Isaiah said to the people of Jerusalem and Judea, he echoed the themes of Amos and Micah. He repeats Micah's message about God judging between the nations and beating "their swords into plowshares and their spears into pruning hooks." He reflects Amos' concern when he challenges the people to "cease to do evil, learn to do good, seek justice, rescue the oppressed, defend the orphan, plead for the widow." Like Amos, he berates the people for worship and sacrifice when they have "blood on their hands" and there is little justice to be found.

Unlike Amos, Hosea and Micah, though, who base their prophetic challenge on Moses and Torah, Isaiah sees God moving among the people through the Davidic monarchy and the worship of the temple. Though no known person appears to fulfill the vision that he spoke to Ahaz, Isaiah speaks in another place of the birth of a royal child. "For a child has been born for us, a son given to us; authority rests upon his shoulders; and he is named Wonderful Counselor, Mighty God, Everlasting Father, Prince of Peace. His authority shall grow continually, and there shall be endless peace for the throne of David and his kingdom. He will establish and uphold it with justice and with righteousness from this time onward and forevermore." We do not know whether Isaiah expected this child in his lifetime or in some distant future. It is clear, however, that he expected the Lord to act through an anointed ruler.

When the Assyrians attacked Jerusalem in the time of Hezekiah, Isaiah advised the king to ignore their threats of destruction. His message was to trust the Lord to deliver Jerusalem from this crisis. Hezekiah accepted Isaiah's counsel and the Assyrians left Jerusalem intact.

When Hezekiah died in 687 BCE, his son, Manasseh, reversed his policies and permitted Assyrian idol worship in the temple. Because Isaiah objected to Manasseh's policies, the king executed him by having him sawn in two.

The next great prophet of Judah, Jeremiah, lived in the time of Josiah's reform (630–609 BCE). He heard the call of God to prophesy when he was very young. Though he objected because of his youth, the Lord set his objections aside and insisted that he take the role of a prophet.

Initially, Jeremiah supported Josiah's reform because of its emphasis on the pure worship of Yahweh. But when the effects of the reform proved to be only a surface change in worship, unaccompanied by any significant change of character among the people, Jeremiah became disenchanted. In 609 BCE, the year of Josiah's death, Jeremiah stood at the entrance of the temple and spoke to the people coming to worship: "Thus says the Lord of hosts, the God of Israel: Amend your ways and your doings, and let me dwell with you in this place. Do not trust in these deceptive words: 'This is the temple of the Lord, the temple of the Lord, the temple of the Lord.'" He told the people in blunt terms that their immoral behavior made their words about the temple a litany of lies. They thought that they could do whatever they wanted and then seek refuge in the temple. Jeremiah challenged them: "Has this house, which is called by my name, become a den of robbers in your sight? You know, I too am watching, says the Lord."

Such words angered the people, particularly the new king, Jehoiakim, and his advisers. To preserve his life, Jeremiah had to go into hiding.

Jeremiah used some of the same themes as Hosea to berate the people of Judah. He looked back to the time of the wilderness wanderings as a time when Israel was devoted to her God, when she walked with him as a loving, faithful wife. Now the people had strayed from faithfulness and "played the whore with many lovers (false gods)." He pleaded with the people to turn away from their sins and establish faithfulness with the Lord again. But his pleas fell on deaf ears.

Jeremiah was a keen observer of the international scene. He saw the growing power of the Babylonians under Nebuchadnezzar. He counseled Jehoiakim not to revolt against Nebuchadnezzar, but the king shunned his advice. He refused to pay tribute and Nebuchadnezzar besieged Jerusalem in 597 BCE. Jehoiachin, Jehoiakim's son and successor, surrendered the city and was taken into exile in Babylon along with the leaders of the nation. Jeremiah wrote to the exiles challenging them to settle down and become a part of the life of Babylon.

The leaders and most of the people of Judah were furious with Jeremiah for such advice. They believed that the exile was God's punishment for the sinfulness of the people before 597 BCE. Now that God's punishment was complete, they wanted to oppose the Babylonians and return the exiles to Judah as soon as possible.

King Zedekiah withheld tribute to the Babylonians in 588 BCE. Nebuchadnezzar led his troops to besiege Jerusalem in the same year. Jeremiah advised Zedekiah to surrender the city and throw himself on the mercy of Nebuchadnezzar. He told Zedekiah that the Lord himself would fight on the side of the Babylonians to destroy the city. For this prophecy, Jeremiah was arrested and thrown into a cistern and kept there for many days. Finally, Zedekiah took pity on him and imprisoned him in the court of the guard.

Jeremiah's prophecy proved accurate. In 586 BCE, the Babylonians broke through Jerusalem's walls and completely destroyed the city and the temple. Zedekiah's sons were killed before him, his eyes were put out, and he was taken to Babylon in chains.

In this time of disaster, the Lord gave Jeremiah a new vision. He had always been concerned for the inner spirit, the heart of the people. He had complained "the sin of Judah is written with an iron pen; with a diamond point it is engraved on the tablet of their hearts..." Now, in a time when the old covenant of Moses had been broken, when the worship life of Israel in the temple had ended, Jeremiah proclaimed that a new day was coming. He spoke of a new covenant that God would make with his people. It would not be like the old covenant, a treaty of outward action and obedience. Speaking for Yahweh, he said: "This is the covenant that I will make with the house of Israel after those days, says the Lord: I will put my law (Torah) within them, and I will write it on their hearts..." The new covenant would be a transformation of character, something Jeremiah saw as the culmination of Torah.

The prophet Ezekiel was a contemporary of Jeremiah. He was taken into exile in Babylon in 597 BCE. There, he had a vision, somewhat like Isaiah's, of the throne chariot of God descending from heaven among the Judeans living by the Chebar River, near Babylon. He described the amazing nature of the throne and the chariot in great detail, but the significance of the vision was that God had abandoned the temple and the people in Judah and had come to be among the exiles.

Ezekiel's overriding concern was for the holiness of God. He saw God acting in history to preserve the sacredness of his name despite the sins of the Israelites, whose major iniquity was profaning Yahweh's name by worshiping other gods.

Ezekiel believed that as long as Yahweh's glory remained in the temple, the temple could not be destroyed. But he had a vision of Yahweh leaving the temple in the same chariot that he had seen coming to the Chebar River. Once Yahweh's glory was gone, Ezekiel knew the temple was doomed.

Ezekiel, however, did not speak only words of judgment. He set aside the long held idea that a person could be punished for the sins of another, especially the idea that God caused children to suffer for their parents' sins. He declared unequivocally that every person would die for his own sin. But if the person would repent, God was ready to forgive. Through Ezekiel, God declared, "I have no pleasure in the death of anyone," meaning that God suffered because of his judgment against sinners.

Holding a belief similar to Jeremiah's, Ezekiel saw the problem of human beings as a problem of inner transformation. God declares through Ezekiel: "A new heart I will give you, and a new spirit I will put within you, and I will remove from your body the heart of stone and give you a heart of flesh. I will put my spirit within you, and make you follow my statutes and be careful to observe my ordinances."

In another vision, God causes Ezekiel to see a valley filled with the dried human bones. He hears God asking, "Son of man, can these bones live?" Ezekiel replied that only God could know whether that were possible. God tells him to speak to the bones, and when he does, the bones come together to form skeletons. Then flesh and skin come on the skeletons and the people live again. God explains this vision as a symbol of the restoration of the whole house of Israel to its land. The people, though dead in their sins and exile, will live again and be restored.

Ezekiel's final vision, extending over the last nine chapters of his book, is a vision of a restored temple whose dimensions surpass in size any building ever constructed. Its grandeur makes it a vision of God's new kingdom, centered on the worship of Israel.

The final prophetic writing that relates historically to the close of the exile and the return of the people to Judah is Isaiah 40—66. The first 39 chapters of Isaiah are mostly about the events surrounding Isaiah's life. These last chapters illuminate God's redemptive activity in bringing his people back to Jerusalem.

The themes of the chapters include God's comfort for his people who languishing in exile, his encouragement for them to return to Judea to reestablish the economic and political nation, and his willingness to form a new relationship with them based on his forgiveness. The opening words of these chapters beautifully express God's compassion, "Comfort, O comfort my people, says your God. Speak tenderly to Jerusalem and cry to her that she has served her term, that her penalty is paid, that she has received from the Lord's hand double for all her sins."

Isaiah sees the Lord leading the people through the wilderness in a new Exodus. They will go with gladness, and God himself will be a shepherd to them. He declares unequivocally that Yahweh, the God of Israel, is the only god that exists, that there are no others. All the nations of the earth are under God's control. He has used the nations in times past to punish Israel. Now God will use the nations to restore the people.

Through Isaiah, God announces that Cyrus is his anointed ruler, his Messiah, to accomplish the release of the exiles. Historically, this is exactly what Cyrus did.

The prophet also mocks the worship of idols, something the people had been a part of in Babylon. He declares that there is nothing at all behind the idols, no divine being whatsoever. The idols are the creation of artisans and nothing more. They are good for nothing except to be burned by fire.

In former times, declares Isaiah, God had related to his people as a Judge because of their sins. Now God is relating to his people as a Redeemer. He will bring them out from their place of punishment. Their redemption will be more than simply a journey home.

There is yet another aspect of this prophetic vision that is unique in the Old Testament. In several passages, the prophet tells of a Servant who will be God's person to carry the message of redemption to the whole earth. Through the prophet, God says of this Servant, "I have taken you by the hand and kept you; I have given you as a covenant to the people, a light to the nations, to open the eyes that are blind, to bring out the prisoners from the dungeon, from the prison those who sit in darkness."

But the task of the Servant will not be accomplished easily. There will be opposition that will ultimately lead to his death, even though he will have done nothing wrong. His death, though, will be redemptive for the sins of others. The Servant will not suffer because of his sins, but because he is willing to give his life that others might be redeemed. As Isaiah puts it, "...the Lord has laid on him the iniquity of us all."

Isaiah never identifies the Servant. He simply tells about his work, his suffering, and the benefit that suffering works in the lives of many others.

With the work of the Servant complete, Isaiah calls the

people to go forth. In a beautiful passage, he states: "For you shall go out in joy and be led back in peace; the mountains and the hills before you shall burst into song, and all the trees of the field shall clap their hands." The historical event is the exodus from Babylon, but the vision encompasses a people going out into the dawn of a bright, eternal day.

The last chapters of Isaiah, 56—66, reflect the situation of the people in the early years after the first exiles returned in 538 BCE. In veiled language, they describe some of the tensions within the community about the political rule and religious practices that should be established. Some of the people wanted to restrict membership in the community only to returning exiles and their descendants. Others felt that God was calling all nations into the fellowship of the Jews. "And the foreigners who join themselves to the Lord, to minister to him, to love the name of the Lord, and to be his servants, all who keep the Sabbath, and do not profane it, and hold fast my covenant—these I will bring to my holy mountain, and make them joyful in my house of prayer, their burnt offerings and their sacrifices will be accepted on my altar; for my house shall be called a house of prayer for all peoples."

There is also a vision of someone with God's spirit and anointing coming to "bring good news to the oppressed, to bind up the broken hearted, to proclaim liberty to the captives, and release to the prisoners; to proclaim the year of the Lord's favor..."

Finally, the prophet sees God bringing in a new realm: "For I am about to create new heavens and a new earth, the former things shall not be remembered or come to mind. But be glad and rejoice forever in what I am creating, for I am about to create Jerusalem as a joy, and its people as a delight."

Yet despite the vision of a divine future, the reality for the returning exiles was a city in ruins, an economy of bare survival, and a temple that could not be used for the worship life of the people. The final three prophets of the Old Testament period, Haggai, Zechariah and Malachi, encouraged the people to rebuild the temple and make the worship practices pure. All three helped to create the expectation that God would intervene in a miraculous way as soon as these tasks were accomplished.

In 515 BCE, the temple was rebuilt and the worship life resumed. Nothing wonderful or miraculous happened. Life went on and Judah remained only a province of the Persian Empire. Though the expectations of Haggai, Zechariah and Malachi were not immediately realized, the people kept the faith of Israel alive while waiting for God to intervene dramatically in world history.

5

A UNIQUE PERSON

The New Testament is the story of a man's life and the beginning of the organization, the Church, which continues to proclaim the meaning of his life. The man was Jesus of Nazareth, later known as Jesus Christ, which means "Jesus who is the Anointed One."

There are four accounts of Jesus' life in the New Testament. Each one is named for its author: Matthew, Mark, Luke and John. The authors were a part of the early Church and all were followers of Jesus. Their accounts differ from one another, though the first three are very similar in structure. John's account differs markedly from the first three. The accounts are called "gospels," which means "good news."

Two of the gospels, Matthew and Luke, begin with stories about Jesus' birth. Though they differ on the details of the story, each of them locates Jesus' birth in Bethlehem, King David's birthplace. Caesar Augustus, the first Roman Emperor, rules the known world. Herod the Great is still the Roman king of Judea. Quirinius is the Roman governor of Syria. Both declare that Mary, Jesus' mother, was a virgin and that his conception was an act of the Holy Spirit of God. Joseph, Mary's husband, is made aware of this by a divinely inspired dream. An angel announces the birth to some shepherds who come to see the baby. Wise men, Persian astrologers, come to visit the child and bring him gifts. Herod hears of Jesus' birth and that he is the King of the Jews and attempts to kill him. Joseph and Mary are forced to flee to Egypt to escape Herod's threat. When they return, they settle in Nazareth, a town in Galilee about 70 miles north of Jerusalem. There, Joseph takes up his trade as a carpenter and other children are born to the family.

When Jesus was twelve years old, his family went to Jerusalem to celebrate the Passover, as was their yearly custom. When the family set out to return, Jesus stayed behind, though Joseph and Mary did not realize it until the end of the first day's journey. The next day, they returned to Jerusalem and searched for him, finally discovering him in the temple, talking to the elders and answering their questions. Mary scolded him for the scare he had given her and Joseph. Jesus simply said that he had to be about his Father's business. Neither Joseph nor Mary understood that he was referring to his relationship with God.

Several years later, when Jesus was about 30 years old, a man named John began preaching by the Jordan River in the wilderness of Judea. He declared that the kingdom of God was coming soon. People came from Jerusalem and the countryside to hear what John was saying. He told them a new age was dawning. It would be so different from the past that only baptism would prepare them for it. Baptism was the way people who were not born Jews were received into Judaism. But John said that even the Jews by birth needed to be baptized to be ready for God's arrival.

Jesus came to the Jordan to hear John and was baptized by him, though John recognized that there was something special about Jesus. John objected at first, saying that he needed to be baptized by Jesus. Jesus insisted and John relented. In the act of

Jesus' baptism, the Holy Spirit came down on him in the form of a dove, a sign that he was God's special man. Jesus then went out into the wilderness where he encountered Satan, God's divine adversary, the personification of evil.

Satan tested Jesus with three challenges. He said that if Jesus really were the Son of God, he could turn stones into bread. Satan encouraged him to jump off the highest peak of the temple wall and trust God to see that he was not hurt by his fall. Finally, he promised that if Jesus worshiped him, he would award him all the kingdoms of the earth. Jesus refused each challenge, or temptation, on the basis of three quotations from Deuteronomy—"One does not live by bread alone, but by every word that comes from the mouth of God;" "Do not put the Lord your God to the test;" and, "Worship the Lord your God, and serve only him."

Shortly after Jesus' temptations, John was arrested for criticizing Herod Antipas, the ruler of Galilee. Sometime following his arrest, Herod executed John for denouncing his marriage to his brother's wife.

When John was arrested, Jesus began preaching in Galilee, saying that the kingdom of God was present and that people should repent and believe this good news. He could say this because his rejection of Satan had demonstrated his power over evil and his special relationship with God.

This declaration was the beginning of Jesus' ministry. We do not know how long his ministry lasted. The gospels are not like biographies that include such details. They are witnesses to Jesus by men who believed he was, indeed, God's Son.

Early in his ministry, Jesus called twelve men to follow him as his disciples or learners. These men traveled with him and he taught them the deeper things about his understanding of God.

Jesus' ministry included acts of healing and the forgiveness of sins. Because of his healings, many people came to see him, listen to him, and have him heal their diseases. The Jewish religious authorities of his time, referred to as "scribes and Pharisees" by the gospel authors, protested that only God could forgive sin and that Jesus had no such authority. Jesus countered their protests by pointing out that his healing miracles proved that he had God's authority with him and that he, therefore, had the right to forgive sins.

Matthew's gospel contains the largest single collection of Jesus' sayings. It is called the Sermon on the Mount. Matthew saw Jesus as a new Moses, delivering a new Torah on a mountain in Galilee. The Sermon began with a series of sayings pronouncing God's blessings on people in various conditions. The blessings were given to the poor in spirit, the mourners, the meek, those who strive to be righteous, the merciful, the pure in heart, the peacemakers, and those who were persecuted for being righteous. Jesus then declared that God's ancient Torah still stood and that not one word of it is unimportant. Jesus spoke of the inner attitudes of those who wanted to follow him. They had to work to resist anger, lust, divorce, and elaborate oaths. They could not turn to violence themselves, even when they were victims of evil. They were to be generous with beggars, an expression of concern for the earth's poor.

Jesus went on to say that his followers should love all the people of the earth, both those whom they considered neighbors and those whom they considered enemies. They should do this because God's nature is to love every person, seeking what is best for each individual.

He then took up the three cardinal acts of pious life for the Jews: the giving of charitable gifts to the poor, prayer and fasting. His message was that his followers should do their charity, their praying and their fasting in secret, rather than being like the religious leaders who made a show of these things. If they did these acts in secret, God would reward them openly.

Jesus challenged his followers not to be overly concerned with the wealth of this world, but to seek to store treasures of a good life in heaven. He told them further not to worry about food, clothing and shelter, because God would provide these things for them, just as he provided for the birds and the grass. Their task, above all else, was to seek God's kingdom and his righteousness and to leave the rest in his hands.

In the closing part of his Sermon, Jesus cautioned his followers to be careful how they judged others, making certain that their own lives were pure. He warned them against giving holy things to people who were not prepared to appreciate them. He told them that God really desired to do good things for those who followed him and that they were to treat others the way they would like to be treated. Finally, he warned them that they could do marvelous things and still miss the kingdom because their eyes were not fixed on him. The consequence of failing to heed this warning was destruction.

After Jesus completed his sermon, he began preaching and healing in the towns of Galilee. Because of the healings and because of his reputation as a man who taught with authority, the crowds became large enough that he met them in the open countryside or on the shores of the Sea of Galilee. Frequently, when he healed people, he would tell them to keep the fact of the healing to themselves.

Much of what he taught the crowds was in the form of parables, stories out of the common life of the people that illustrated some point about the kingdom of God. For example, he told a story about a farmer who sowed his seed. Some of the seed fell on the path and was eaten by birds. Some fell on rocky ground, where it grew quickly and then died just as quickly because it did not get enough water. Some fell among weeds that came up and choked the life from the young plants. But some of the seed fell on good soil and yielded as much as a hundred times the amount of seed sown. The gospels interpret the parable as a reference to the good news of Jesus' presence, the seed, and the soils as the various kinds of people who hear the good news. The most remarkable thing about the parable is the incredible return on the seed in good soil. Most farmers considered a crop of ten times the amount of seed excellent. Such a bountiful harvest is a clear symbol of the presence of God's kingdom.

Other parables of Jesus illustrate the nature of God, particularly his mercy and his longing to reach out to the lost people of the world—those with no hope of anything but grinding poverty or sin in this life. Some stories emphasized the nearness of the kingdom and the necessity to be on the lookout for God's coming and to be ready to join him when he did come. Some challenged people to be faithful with the gifts that God had given them in this life because there would be an accounting when the Lord came. Some parables warned the people of God's judgment on those who had not ignored his prophets and even put them to death because they did not like the words the prophets spoke.

One of the miracles that Jesus performed, recorded in all four gospels, is the feeding of the 5,000. After John's execution, Jesus took his disciples to the eastern side of the Sea of Galilee. But the crowds followed and remained with him all day while he taught them and healed the sick. As evening approached, Jesus' disciples told him to send the crowd away so that they could find something to eat. Jesus told his disciples to give the people food. They pointed to the thousands of people and told him they had only five loaves of bread and two small fish. Jesus took the loaves and the fish, blessed them, and told the disciples to distribute them to the people. When all the people had been fed, there were still twelve baskets full of food left over.

Jesus was not, however, universally popular. The Pharisees became upset with him because he was not careful about observing all of the narrow laws and prohibitions that related to the Sabbath. They thought that if all the Jews kept the Sabbath precisely for even one day, the kingdom of God would come immediately. On one occasion, for example, Jesus was in a synagogue on the Sabbath when a man with a withered arm came in. Jesus healed his arm, but the Pharisees were furious. According to their law, it was not legal to heal on the Sabbath unless it was a matter of life or death. They left the synagogue and conspired with Herod's officials about getting rid of Jesus.

Unlike the Pharisees, the political authorities, particularly the Romans, were not concerned about the religious debates within Judaism. What did concern them, though, was the fact that several men, contemporaries of Jesus, had proclaimed themselves God's Messiah. Each of them had led an uprising against Rome that had been brutally suppressed. Jesus himself never raised the standard of revolt, but the Romans were suspicious of him and ready to put him to death at the slightest provocation.

Later, Jesus was traveling through the northern part of Galilee. There, he asked his disciples what people were saying about him. They replied that many were saying that he was John the Baptist come back to life. Others said that he was Elijah, Jeremiah or one of the other prophets. Then Jesus asked them directly who *they* thought he was. Simon, the fisherman, responded: "You are the Messiah, the Son of the living God." Because of his statement, Jesus gave Simon the name Peter ("Rock.") On the conviction of faith expressed by Peter, he would establish a group of "set-apart persons" (the meaning of the word translated "church"). He then ordered the disciples not to tell anyone else that he was the Messiah.

After that, Jesus began to tell the disciples that he had to go to Jerusalem to proclaim his gospel in the capital city of Judaism. He foresaw that his proclamation would not be accepted and that the authorities would turn against him and execute him by crucifixion, the standard Roman method of capital punishment. Jesus added that three days later, he would be raised from the dead. Peter objected that such an outcome could never happen to the Messiah. Jesus told him that he was speaking as Satan would speak and not as God would speak.

Jesus then declared to all of his disciples: "If any want to become my followers, let them deny themselves, and take up their cross and follow me. For those who want to save their life will lose it, and those who lose their life for my sake will find it."

Shortly after this, Jesus took three of his disciples—Peter, James and John—and went up a high mountain. There Jesus' whole appearance was illumined and the disciples saw Moses and Elijah talking with him. They heard the voice of God saying, "This is my Son…listen to him." With that, the vision was complete and they saw only Jesus. Jesus commanded the three not to tell anyone about this incident until he had been raised from the dead.

Jesus set out with his disciples to go to Jerusalem to celebrate the Passover, the Jewish feast recalling the Exodus from Egypt. On the way, he stopped at the home of Mary and Martha in Bethany, a village near Jerusalem. Their brother had died four days earlier and the sisters were troubled because they felt Jesus could have cured his illness. Jesus raised their brother, Lazarus, from the dead, a miracle so extraordinary that the high priest feared the whole nation would follow Jesus. Better that Jesus die, he felt, than that the whole nation be turned upside down.

As Jesus and his disciples came close to the city, his disciples found a donkey for him to ride into Jerusalem. They came down the Mount of Olives waving palm branches and shouting, "Hosanna to the Son of David! Blessed is the one who comes in the name of the Lord!" This action related to a saying in Zechariah that Jerusalem's deliverer would come humbly, riding on a donkey, symbolizing his peaceful intention rather than riding a horse, a beast of war.

After he entered the city, Jesus went to the temple and encountered the moneychangers converting money from all over the world into the currency of the temple. Worshipers could only purchase animals for sacrifice with temple money. He knew the exchange rates unfairly favored those who provided the temple cash. Jesus was so infuriated that he led his disciples, and others who joined them, in driving the moneychangers out of the temple, saying, "My house shall be called a house of prayer for all nations, but you are making it a den of robbers." This action turned the temple authorities completely against him. They began immediately to plan for his arrest and execution.

For each of the next three days, Jesus came to the temple to teach the people. The religious authorities were afraid to arrest him because he had won over the crowds. He answered questions about his authority and about whether or not to pay taxes. He chastised the scribes and the Pharisees for being hypocrites, performing their religious observances for show while ignoring the situation of the poor in the land. He also spoke of the coming of a day of judgment when God would strike the earth and all people would be brought before the throne of the Son of Man to be rewarded for their righteousness or damned for their wickedness. The righteous would enter God's eternal kingdom and the wicked would be eternally punished.

The authorities decided to arrest Jesus at night, but needed someone able to lead them to where he might be and identify him. One of his disciples, Judas Iscariot, was willing to betray Jesus for money.

On Thursday evening, the night of the Passover meal, Jesus sent his disciples ahead of him to prepare a place for them to eat. They found a large, upstairs room and made preparations there. During the meal, Jesus announced that one of them would betray him. All the disciples were shocked. Each one exclaimed, "Not I!"

While they were eating, Jesus broke a loaf of bread and said, "Take, eat; this is my body." Then he took a cup of wine and said, "Drink from it, all of you, for this is my blood of the covenant, which is poured out for many for the forgiveness of sins."

After the supper, Judas left to join the authorities who had planned to arrest Jesus. The rest of his disciples followed Jesus to an olive garden called Gethsemane, located just outside the walls of Jerusalem. There, Jesus asked Peter, James and John to sit with him while he prayed. He pleaded with God not to die. No answer came. Jesus finally submitted to God's will for him.

After Jesus' plea to God, he found the disciples sleeping and told them to get up so they could leave. Before they could get out of the garden, Judas and a company of the temple guards arrived. Judas kissed Jesus to identify him and the guards arrested him and took him to the high priest's house.

The high priest, Caiaphas, had summoned an unusual nighttime meeting of the council of the Jews to try Jesus. Evidently, Caiaphas was determined to dispose of Jesus quickly. They brought witnesses against him who reported he had threatened to destroy the temple. But their testimony was contradictory. Finally, Caiaphas asked Jesus directly: "Are you the Messiah, the Son of the Blessed One?" Jesus answered, "I am." At this, the high priest exclaimed that he had committed blasphemy in declaring himself to be like God. He said that Jesus deserved to die and the council agreed with him.

In the morning, they took Jesus to Pontus Pilate, the Roman

governor. Pilate was not concerned about the religious issues of Jesus' case, but he did ask Jesus if he was the king of the Jews. Jesus did not answer him and Pilate was inclined to let him go. But the high priest's people had stirred up the crowd to demand that Jesus be crucified. Wanting to avoid a riot and uncertain about whether Jesus would become the focal point of a revolt, Pilate gave in and ordered that Jesus be crucified.

The Roman soldiers took Jesus, beat him, and then led him and two thieves to the place of the skull, Golgotha, outside the city walls. There they stripped him, nailed his arms and feet to the cross, did the same to the thieves, and set the three crosses in the earth with Jesus in the middle.

Jesus' disciples, fearing for their lives, ran and left him. Peter even denied three times that he knew Jesus, fulfilling one of Jesus' predictions.

Jesus hung on the cross from nine in the morning until three in the afternoon. One of the thieves cursed him repeatedly. The other pleaded with Jesus to remember him when Jesus came into his kingdom. Jesus promised that the thief would be with him.

About three o'clock, Jesus cried out: "My God, my God! Why have you forsaken me?" Some of those who were standing near the cross thought he was calling for Elijah. It was Jesus' final cry. Moments later, he breathed his last.

Joseph of Arimathea, a secret follower of Jesus, asked Pilate for his body. Pilate gave Joseph permission to remove Jesus' body from the cross. Joseph wrapped the body in a linen cloth and laid it in a cave tomb. He rolled a stone over the door to seal the tomb until Jesus' body could be anointed.

Because the day following Jesus' death was the Sabbath, no one came to the tomb to anoint his body for burial rites.

Very early on the first day of the week, our Sunday, three women—Mary Magdalene, Mary, the mother of James, and

Salome—brought spices to anoint his body. When they arrived at the tomb, they found the stone had been rolled away from the entrance. Jesus' body was gone. A young man in a white robe was sitting in the cave. The young man told them not to be frightened. Jesus had risen from the dead and was going to Galilee, where he would see them along with Peter and the other disciples.

This story of Jesus' resurrection is found in Mark's gospel. The other gospels include differing stories of Jesus appearing to his disciples and others after his resurrection. Matthew tells that Jesus went to Galilee before the disciples and met them on a mountain there. He challenged them to "make disciples of all nations, baptizing them in the name of the Father and of the Son and of the Holy Spirit." He promised he would always be with them.

Luke tells of Jesus walking with two men who were going to the little town of Emmaus. They had heard rumors about his resurrection, but they did not believe them and they did not recognize him. Jesus interpreted the prophetic saying for them so that they would understand he had to rise from the dead. Still, they did not know him until they sat in an inn after their journey and ate with them. Jesus disappeared and later met his disciples in Jerusalem, where he showed them the wounds on his hands and feet. He shared a meal of fish with them. Then, he took his disciples out as far as Bethany and, as he was blessing them, he was taken up to heaven.

John's gospel reports Jesus' encounter with Mary Magdalene at the entrance of the tomb, where his friends had laid his body. At first, Mary did not recognize him through her tears. Then, Jesus said her name and she knew who he was. Later that day, Jesus met his disciples in a closed room and breathed the Holy Spirit upon them. One of the disciples, Thomas, who was called "the Twin," was not present. Later, when his companions told him of Jesus' being with them, he said that he would not believe such a thing unless he saw Jesus for himself and felt the wounds in his hands, feet and side.

A week later, according to John, Jesus appeared again to his disciples and challenged Thomas to see for himself. Thomas believed and called Jesus his Lord and God.

John's gospel closes with a story of the resurrected Jesus meeting his disciples by the Sea of Galilee after they had spent an unsuccessful night fishing. Jesus called out to them from the shore and told them to cast their nets on the other side of the boat. They caught so many fish that they could hardly haul in the net. Peter recognized that the man on the shore was Jesus and jumped out of the boat to go to him. Three times Jesus asked Peter if he loved him, corresponding to Peter's three denials. Then Jesus told him to "Feed my sheep," meaning to go and teach those who would follow Jesus in the days and years to come. After this instruction to Peter, Jesus left them.

6

OUT OF THIS WORLD

Luke wrote a second volume, Acts, which is included in the New Testament. It is the story of what happened after the resurrection of Jesus, explaining how the early church developed.

Acts begins with the account of the final encounter between Jesus and his eleven disciples. (Judas, who betrayed Jesus, killed himself.) Jesus told the disciples that they should stay in Jerusalem until the power of the Holy Spirit came upon them. When he finished telling them what to do, he was taken up to heaven and the disciples did not see him again.

Peter told the disciples that they should choose a man to replace Judas, since the number twelve was significant to Israel and to Jesus. After praying about the choice, they chose between Matthias and Justus by "casting lots," something like rolling dice. Matthias was chosen.

Fifty days after Passover, there was a Jewish festival in Jerusalem called Pentecost. It was a celebration of God's giving the Torah on Mt. Sinai. The disciples and other followers of Jesus were all together praying when the house was filled with the sound of a mighty wind. Flames appeared, with one flame resting on each of them. They were filled with the Holy Spirit and began to speak in other languages by the power of the Spirit.

As they went out into the street, a large crowd gathered around them because it was obvious that something strange had occurred. Since people from all over the Roman Empire were in Jerusalem for Pentecost, many different languages were represented among the people. But each person heard Jesus' followers telling about God's deeds and power in his or her own language. At first, they thought Jesus' followers were drunk. But Peter, speaking for the apostles, reminded them that it was only 9:00 AM and that it was too early to be drunk. He went on to explain that what they were seeing was the coming of the Holy Spirit as predicted by the prophet Joel: "In the last days it will be, God declares, that I will pour out my Spirit upon all flesh, and your sons and your daughters shall prophesy, and your young men shall see visions, and your old men shall dream dreams." He went on to relate the event to Jesus' life, death and, particularly, the resurrection. Jesus' resurrection showed that he was the Messiah whom, David had predicted, "The Lord said to my Lord, 'Sit at my right hand until I make your enemies your footstool.'"

The people listening were astounded and deeply grieved at what Peter said. They asked what they should do. Peter replied, "Repent, and be baptized every one of you in the name of Jesus Christ so that your sins may be forgiven; and you will receive the gift of the Holy Spirit." About 3,000 people were baptized that day. Peter had proclaimed that through the crucifixion and resurrection of Jesus, all who believed and repented received forgiveness of sins and the power of the Holy Spirit.

From this beginning, the church grew in numbers. There was little formal organization. Peter, James and John were the principal leaders of the work. They were joined by James, the brother of Jesus, who became leader of the church in Jerusalem. All of the early followers of Jesus (called "followers of the Way") were Jews.

At first, the religious and political authorities ignored the church. Then the arrests of the apostles began. They were taken before the Council because they had healed many people in Jesus' name and preached about the resurrection. The Council wanted to put them to death, but a wise teacher, Gamaliel, advised against it. He said that if what the apostles were doing were against God's will, it would eventually fade away. If it were God's will, nothing they could do would stop it. So the Council had the apostles flogged and then released them. They returned immediately to proclaiming Jesus as the Messiah.

In the early days of the church, believers sometimes gave their property to the control of the church in order to provide for the widows and other poor persons. The work of administering this part of the church became too much for the apostles, so they appointed seven men as deacons to oversee the distribution of food while the apostles focused on prayer and preaching.

Stephen, one of the deacons, performed many wonders and spoke with great power about Jesus. Some of the Jews complained to the elders and the scribes, even providing false witnesses who accused Stephen of saying Jesus would destroy the Temple and change the customs of Moses. They put him on trial before the high priest. Stephen preached a fiery sermon declaring that the Jewish authorities had killed the Righteous One of God, Jesus. This so incensed his listeners that they condemned him to death, dragged him outside the city and stoned him. A young man named Saul held the coats of those who threw the stones and he approved of their killing Stephen.

A great persecution broke out against the church in Jerusalem and the apostles were scattered throughout the land. They continued to proclaim Jesus wherever they went. One of them, Philip, preached about Jesus in Samaria and healed many people while in that city. When he left Samaria, Philip went south and encountered an Ethiopian official returning from Jerusalem. Philip heard him reading a passage from Isaiah. He interpreted the passage for him and the official asked to be baptized.

Meanwhile, Saul was still incensed at the followers of Jesus. Because he was a very well educated Jew and highly respected for his age, he asked the Jerusalem authorities for a letter authorizing him to go to Damascus to arrest Jesus' followers there. He promised he would bring them back to Jerusalem for trial. While on the way to Damascus with some soldiers to help him arrest Christians, a light from the sky flashed around him. The light was so bright he fell to the ground. He heard a voice ask, "Saul, Saul, why do you persecute me?" He asked who was speaking and the voice replied, "I am Jesus, whom you are persecuting." Jesus told him to get up and go into the city and he would be told what to do. When Saul stood up, he was blind, and his traveling companions had to lead him to Damascus.

After three days, the Lord, in a vision, directed Ananias, one of the believers in Damascus, to go to Saul and lay hands on him to heal his eyes. Ananias objected because he had heard of Saul's mission. The Lord insisted because he had chosen Saul to be an apostle for him. Ananias went, laid his hands on Saul, and he was healed. Saul was baptized and immediately began to proclaim Jesus as the Son of God in the synagogues of Damascus. This angered the Jews so much that they plotted to kill him. Saul escaped from Damascus by being lowered in a basket through a window in the wall. He then went to Jerusalem and Barnabas introduced him to the apostles. Again, Saul argued with the Jews who were against the new movement. They attempted to kill him, so his new friends took him to Caesarea and, from there, he went to live in Tarsus.

Luke tells a story about a Roman Centurion named Cornelius who lived in Caesarea and had become a believer in the God of Judaism. He was known as a devout man who prayed faithfully. One day, an angel appeared before him and told him to send men to Joppa to bring Peter back to Caesarea. Cornelius obeyed and sent two slaves and a soldier to bring Peter to Caesarea.

Just before the men from Cornelius arrived at the house where Peter was staying, Peter had a vision. Three times he saw a sheet, suspended at each corner, coming down from heaven. In it were all kinds of four-footed creatures, reptiles and birds. Each time he heard God tell him to get up, kill and eat. Each time, Peter, a devout Jew, refused because he considered the creatures unclean and forbidden by Jewish law. God told Peter that what he called clean Peter ought not call profane. While Peter was still trying to figure out what the vision meant, the men from Cornelius arrived. God told Peter to go with them because he had sent for him.

Peter went to Cornelius' house. Cornelius wanted to worship him, but Peter told him that he was only a man. Peter then realized his vision meant that he should not hesitate to speak to these Roman gentiles (non-Jews) even though it was against Jewish law for him to be in Cornelius' house and associate with him. Peter began to preach about Jesus Christ. While he was still speaking, the Holy Spirit came over all who were there and they began to speak in different languages. At this evidence that the Holy Spirit could come even to gentiles, Peter baptized Cornelius and his household and stayed with them for several days.

When Peter returned to Jerusalem, the apostles there rejoiced that "God had given even to the gentiles the repentance that leads to life." Some of the leaders of the church had been forced to flee Jerusalem by the persecution following Stephen's stoning. Several of them went to Antioch, one of the leading cities of the eastern Mediterranean. They proclaimed Christ to the Jews of the city and were successful in attracting many. Barnabas was in Antioch and, seeing the increasing number of followers of Christ, he went to Tarsus to find Saul. He brought him to Antioch. In Antioch, the believers were first called "Christians." It may have been a derisive term. Jesus' disciples were first called "followers of The Way."

King Herod of Jerusalem now began to persecute the church. The year was 43 CE (Common Era). He executed James, John's brother, and had Peter thrown in prison. But Peter miraculously escaped, and, because of the continuing danger, he went to Caesarea.

Sometime around 48 CE, the church in Antioch commissioned Barnabas and Saul (who from this point is called "Paul," the Roman version of Saul) as missionaries to travel and spread the good news of Jesus Christ. They went first to Cyprus and from there sailed to Asia Minor, the land we know today as Turkey. They took John Mark, a cousin of Barnabas, with them. He stayed with them until they arrived in Asia Minor and then he left to return to Antioch.

When they arrived in a town where they wanted to preach, they would go to the synagogue and proclaim the good news of Christ to the Jews. Some would believe, but many, usually including the rulers of the synagogue, would not. Paul and Barnabas would then go to the gentiles in the town and many of them would be persuaded. Their success among the gentiles would anger the Jews who would incite the prominent people and leaders of the community against them. Several times Paul and Barnabas were driven forcefully out of the towns they visited. In one instance, the people of the community stoned Paul and dragged him outside the city, leaving him for dead. But he survived the attack and left for another city.

Thus, churches were established in towns throughout Asia Minor, particularly in locations of commerce where there would be an opportunity to tell travelers about Jesus Christ. In each place, Paul would appoint elders who would guide the church in its worship and organization.

After the journey, Paul and Barnabas returned to Antioch. After awhile, some men from Judea came to Antioch and began to teach the Christians there that unless they were circumcised and began to follow the Law of Moses, they could not be saved. This meant that in order to be fully Christian, gentiles must also become Jews. Paul and Barnabas strongly opposed this idea. Paul, who was well versed in the Law, recognized that the Law had never done for him what Jesus Christ had done: saved him from the Law that led to death. He saw the church as a sign of the new age of God, uniting both Jews and gentiles in a new community of faith in Christ.

Since the dispute could not be resolved in Antioch, Paul and Barnabas and some others were sent to Jerusalem to get a ruling from the leaders of the church there. Peter was present at the gathering along with James, the brother of Jesus. Peter told the story of his experience with Cornelius. Paul and Barnabas told of what had happened on their missionary journey and that many gentiles had become Christians as a result.

After considerable discussion, James spoke to the whole assembly and said that gentiles should not be required to be circumcised or to observe the whole Law of Moses. The council wrote a letter saying: "For it has seemed good to the Holy Spirit and to us to impose on you [gentiles] no further burden than these essentials: that you abstain from what has been sacrificed to idols and from blood and from what is strangled and from fornication." The restrictions had to do with separating Christians from practices related to the worship of idols among the Greeks and Romans. They were, however, expected to conduct their lives in accordance with the moral laws of the Torah.

Paul and Barnabas returned to Antioch and published the decision of the Jerusalem Council. After some time, Paul decided that he wanted to make another missionary journey and visit the churches that he and Barnabas had established. Barnabas insisted on taking his cousin, John Mark, with them. Paul objected and Barnabas refused to go with him. So Paul chose Silas and they set off.

During this journey, Paul went to Philippi, a Roman colony and important city in Macedonia. There, he established a church. But Paul's activities interfered with the business of some of the citizens of Philippi. These people brought him before the courts and accused him of encouraging practices that were not lawful for Romans. Paul and his companions were beaten and thrown in jail. That night, there was an earthquake so violent that all the jail's doors came open and the prisoners' chains fell off. Since the jailer would be executed if he lost a prisoner, he was about to kill himself. Paul stopped him and told him that all the prisoners were accounted for. The jailer was so overwhelmed that he and his whole family became Christians.

The next day, the magistrates were going to let Paul go free, but he insisted that they escort him because he was a Roman citizen and had been unjustly beaten and jailed. Fearful that Paul might report their wrongdoing, they did as he asked.

Paul and Silas left Philippi and proceeded to Athens, the cultural and intellectual center of the world. There, Paul had a chance to speak at the Areopagus, a place of assembly where the Athenians gathered to hear about the latest philosophical or religious development. Paul related the God of the Jews to a statue in Athens dedicated to an "Unknown God." He concluded that this God had fixed a day for judging the world by a man whom he had sent (Jesus), and whom God had raised from the dead. Some of the Athenians believed. Others were deeply skeptical.

From Athens, Paul went to Corinth, where he established a church. Corinth was a seaport city with a reputation for immorality. Paul determined to emphasize nothing among the Corinthians except Christ crucified and raised from the dead. He preached the good news to both Jews and gentiles, while remaining in Corinth for a year-and-a-half. He then visited Ephesus, a great seaport, and from there sailed to Caesarea. He visited Jerusalem and returned to Antioch where he stayed for some time.

Paul made one more missionary journey, visiting many of the places where he had established churches. While he was in Ephesus, one of the Ephesian silversmiths, who had made his living selling statues of the goddess Diana, complained that Paul had preached that man-made gods were worthless. He stirred up the citizens of Ephesus against Paul and the Christians. The town clerk, a leading man of the city, prevented a riot.

Paul continued on his journey. On the return trip, he asked the elders of the Ephesian church to meet him on the shore at Miletus. There, Paul said a poignant farewell to them because he had a premonition that he would not see them again. He challenged them to tend the flock, the congregation, in Ephesus. Then he knelt in prayer with them and they wept together.

Paul returned to Jerusalem via Caesarea, feeling all the while that a crisis awaited him in Jerusalem. When he arrived, the apostles greeted him and told him that there was great anger with him among the Jews. Many believed that Paul had been teaching Jews to abandon the practices of Judaism and accept Jesus as the Messiah. The leaders of the Jerusalem church encouraged him to go through a Jewish ritual of purification to counter the rumors. Before the completion of the ritual, Jews from Asia arrived in Jerusalem, recognized Paul, and stirred up the crowd against him. The Roman authorities came and arrested Paul. They gave him a chance to speak to the crowd, but the crowd still wanted him dead. The Romans were about to punish him by flogging, but Paul invoked his Roman citizenship and they halted the proceedings.

The next day, the Jewish authorities plotted to have Paul assassinated. Paul heard about it and informed the Romans who took him under armed guard to Caesarea. The governor heard his case, but was reluctant to decide it and kept him in prison for two years. When a new governor, Festus, was appointed, he heard the Jews' case against Paul. Festus planned to send him to Jerusalem for trial, but Paul, on the basis of his Roman citizenship, appealed his case to the Emperor.

Shortly after his appeal, King Agrippa, who ruled parts of Palestine, came to Caesarea to visit Festus. Festus made arrangements to have Paul speak in his own defense before himself and Agrippa. Paul recounted the story of his encounter with Jesus Christ on the Road to Damascus. Agrippa and Festus agreed that Paul had done nothing wrong, but because he had appealed his case to the Emperor, they had to send him to Rome.

Paul was put on a ship bound for Rome. The ship ran into a storm at sea and finally was wrecked on the coast of the island of Malta. Everyone survived. Three months later, they set sail again on another ship that had wintered at Malta and arrived in Rome. Paul was placed under house arrest and waited two years for the Emperor to hear his case.

The book of Acts ends at this point. Many people believe that Paul's case went against him and that he was executed sometime in 63 CE, during the reign of Emperor Nero.

Besides the Gospels and Acts, the New Testament includes 21 letters, the majority of them written by Paul, and the Book of Revelation, a writing that is a vision of the end of this world and the beginning of a new heaven and a new earth. The letters are especially important because they tell about the challenges faced by the early church, particularly the congregations that Paul helped establish. Paul also wrote a letter to the church at Rome (Romans), introducing himself and setting forth his understanding of the nature of the Christian faith.

In Romans, Paul argues that all people "have sinned and fallen short of the glory of God." Paul himself had tried to become right with God by zealously keeping the Torah, but he had failed. He discovered righteousness with God only when he encountered the risen Christ on the road to Damascus. He believed that his sins had been forgiven through what Jesus Christ had done in his sacrifice on the cross. This conviction was verified by Jesus' resurrection from the dead. He further believed that what Jesus had done transcended the Torah and that salvation in Christ was available to all people, both Jews and gentiles. He anchored this belief on a sentence from the prophet Habakkuk: "The one who is righteous will live by faith." He contrasted this righteousness that came through faith in Christ to the keeping of the Torah, which never made anyone righteous before God.

But faith in Jesus was something more than simply intellectual assent to a set of beliefs. As Paul put it, the believer was "to 'put on' the Lord Jesus Christ." By this, he meant that those who followed Jesus were to become like him. This would be accomplished by the Holy Spirit working in the life of him who has faith in Christ. Said simply, Christians were to become "little Christs."

Paul recognized that there was a danger that those who believed in Christ might so disregard the Law that they would believe they could do whatever they liked. He had preached that where there was much sin, God's grace had come abundantly in Christ to overcome sin. Since this was so, some might reason, why not go on sinning so that God's grace would be made even more available.

Paul's answer was that believers had, in a sense, died to sin with Christ. And how could anyone "who had died to sin go on living in it?" Faith in Christ, according to Paul, makes us more and more able to live lives of righteousness and be better than the Law requires. Anyone who thinks he can believe in Christ and go on sinning has missed the point of Christ's coming and dying so that sin might be forgiven.

For Paul, the church was to be a community of believers whose lives together would be the light of Christ for the pagan world. The church would be the "body of Christ" in the world. They were to be zealous — glowing with the

Spirit and serving the Lord. They would rejoice in hope, show patience in suffering, persevere in prayer and extend hospitality to strangers. In all of this, the members of the church would be imitators of Paul as Paul was an imitator of Christ.

In one of his letters to the church in Corinth, Paul spoke eloquently about the spiritual gifts that had become available to believers in Jesus. He gave them a simple test to tell who had received the Holy Spirit: "No one can say 'Jesus is Lord' except by the Holy Spirit." The phrase meant that Jesus was the Lord of heaven and earth, the same as Yahweh.

Paul then went on to describe the attributes of the love that should be present among Christian believers. "Love is patient; love is kind; love is not envious or boastful or arrogant or rude. It does not insist on its own way, it is not irritable or resentful; it does not rejoice in wrongdoing, but rejoices in the truth. It bears all things, believes all things, hopes all things, endures all things. Love never ends." In the age in which Jesus and Paul lived, such characteristics were extremely rare and seldom practiced.

New Testament letters, other than Paul's, describe the development of the early church and the various offices of those who were called by God to lead the church. They encourage believers to keep the faith even in the face of persecution. Because Christians believed that only Jesus was Lord, they refused to say that Caesar (the Emperor) was Lord, something required by the Romans of all people who lived under their authority. Because of their refusal, many Christians were put to death in the first three centuries of the life of the church.

The letter to the Hebrews identifies Jesus as the final High Priest of the Hebrew faith. It pictures Jesus entering into the holiest place in the temple to make the supreme sacrifice of his own body, thereby forever doing away with the sacrificial system of Judaism.

Revelation, the last book of the Bible, tells in vivid images about the final battle between the forces of Satan and the forces of the Lord. When the battle is over, all the people of the world appear before Jesus, returning in triumph, for judgment. Heaven and earth, as we know them, come to an end. A new heaven and a new earth appear, centered on a glorified, heavenly Jerusalem that comes down "like a bride dressed for her husband." The faithful in Christ will live eternally in this everlasting city.

7

POST SCRIPT

The story is complete. The Good News of the life, death and resurrection of Jesus of Nazareth, God's Messiah, rooted in and fulfilling the story of the people of Israel, lives in our world today. Though we are more than 2000 years from the birth of Jesus, by the power of the Holy Spirit, his presence is still alive in the hearts of millions of his followers around the world. Most of these faithful, humble people will be known only to a few and their lives, when over, will soon be forgotten. They call themselves "Christians," but they do it gently, never with bombast or an attitude of superiority.

These Christians are very conscious that this world is not their real home. They believe that their lives are important and that their Savior guides them to live according to his will for them. They discover that will mostly by reading the Bible and becoming more knowledgeable about its story. They see their lives as a time and space extension of the lives of that original band of believers who experienced, firsthand, the presence of the risen Christ and the coming of the Holy Spirit. But they recognize that their earthly existence is only a pilgrimage toward their permanent dwelling, the place where Jesus is, where they will be with him and with one another. They live as strangers and aliens on this earth. If they are citizens of an earthly nation, they know that condition is only temporary. The nation, indeed the whole earth, is a dying husk, soon to be discarded and forgotten.

Paradoxically, they do not despair of the worldly human situation. They believe that Jesus Christ came to save the world one person at a time. That the sun may burn out and the universe might finally collapse upon itself are not matters of great concern. Human beings, redeemed by Christ, will outlive the universe. It is not the temporary physical earth or other physical worlds that are the focus of God's concern. The real realm of God lies beyond the physical. Though it can be entered partially in the present time, it can be entered fully only through death, transformed by the resurrection of Jesus Christ. In that resurrection, these simple Christians all participate. Their earthly experience will not be blotted out, but will be transformed, "translated into a better language," as John Donne so poetically put it.

While they endure their earthly life, true believers add a fresh savor to the communities in which they dwell. Sometimes, they are persecuted for their beliefs. When they are so abused, they do not retaliate. They bless their tormenters and pray for their redemption. They care for the hungry. They are present to those in despair. They reach out to people who have lost any hope that life will ever mean anything. While their neighbors may curse their earthly circumstances, Christians are quick to bless and to encourage. They risk their lives to give help to the helpless. They shed tears with the grieving, and rejoice with those who celebrate.

In simple fact, these humble people become an ongoing part of the biblical story. By their lives, they make the Bible a living book. They are the light set on a hill so others can see their good works and praise their heavenly Father. Their actions are a witness about the Lord whom they follow. This living witness encourages others to join their company. And so the Church has grown as the years have passed.

Some day, some people suggest, the company of believers in Jesus Christ will dwindle and disappear. Many think it is an antiquated story that has outlived its usefulness — that it comes from the age of superstition, the age before human beings learned the massive amount of information we now possess about our physical world. Some people talk about "man coming of age," now mature enough so that we no longer need stories about God and a divine person walking upon the earth. Human beings, so they think, can handle their own problems without any help from any deity. They may be correct, but the recent history does not indicate any increasing ability to deal creatively with the problems of people and nations. On the contrary, the conflicts and catastrophes of human making—the wars, the starvation of hundreds of thousands, the genocides of recent times, the intransigence of governments and the foolishness of national leaders —all indicate that we are no more able to handle our problems today than we were when our ancient ancestors first crawled out of caves.

In the face of all of this, humble Christians live their faith. They labor quietly to save the world from disaster. They never despair. They pray fervently for Jesus Christ to come again and establish an eternal kingdom of light, joy, peace and love.

ABOUT THE AUTHOR

Dr. J. Michael Miller graduated from the U.S. Naval Academy in 1956 and served as a Naval Officer for eight years, mostly on submarines. After leaving the Navy, he attended Boston University School of Theology and Graduate School, earning a PhD in Biblical Studies, Old Testament. He served churches in Massachusetts, Illinois and Georgia. For seven years, he was an Assistant Professor of Old Testament at Oral Roberts University School of Theology.

Dr. Miller passed away in July 2015. He is remembered far and wide for his intelligence, his sense of humor, and his ability to challenge and teach, making the message of the Bible relevant to daily life.

Learn more about this amazing man in the book *Fair Winds and Following Seas: Remembering Mike Miller* .